# The Perimeter
# Attack Offense:
# Key to Winning Football

# THE PERIMETER
# ATTACK OFFENSE:
# KEY TO WINNING FOOTBALL

Joseph H. Moglia

Parker Publishing Company, Inc.

West Nyack, New York

© 1982, by

PARKER PUBLISHING COMPANY, INC.

West Nyack, N.Y.

**Library of Congress Cataloging in Publication Data**

Moglia, Joseph H.
    Perimeter attack offense.

    Includes index.
    1. Football—Offense.   2. Football coaching.
I. Title.
GV951.8.M63        796.332'2        81-11242
ISBN 0-13-657221-9        AACR2

Printed in the United States of America

# DEDICATION

For putting up with my being away from home so often, and for putting up with my pre-season, in-season, and post-season moods and anxieties: but most of all, for always trying to be there when I need them; this book is dedicated to my wife, three daughters, and son:

Kathe

Kelly Ann

Kimberly Patrice

Kara Theresa

Kevin Joseph

It is also dedicated to the boys I have coached, as well as the men I have worked with, each of whom has worked hard to be a man and to develop men. Alphabetically, the men who have worked with me, or for whom I have worked, follow:

Gary Anderson (Penncrest)
Rev. M. Avicolli (Archmere)
Bruce Bott (Fordham)
Paul Boudreau (Dartmouth)
Bruce Carter (Penncrest)
John Curtis (Dartmouth)
Bill Doyle (Archmere)
Jim Feddeck (Fordham)
Al Haddad (Lafayette)
Frank Hershey (Dartmouth)

Curtis Jones (Dartmouth)
John Justo (Lafayette)
Frank Kennedy (Lafayette)
George Landis (Dartmouth)
Tom Lewis (Archmere)
Lou Maranzana (Dartmouth)
Bernie McFadden (Archmere)
Ed Michener (Lafayette)
Rev. O.J. Mullen (Archmere)
Norm Muro (Fordham)

John Piper (Lafayette)  Garry Scutt (Lafayette)
Doug Pollard (Lafayette)  Jack Signor (Penncrest)
Paul Pomeroy (Archmere)  Bob Sior (Fordham)
Neil Putnam (Lafayette)  Bill Smith (Penncrest)
Dennis Roccia (Penncrest)  Paul Spahr (Penncrest)
Joe Sarra (Lafayette)  Sonny Yarnell (Penncrest)
Mike Scheetz (Penncrest)  Joe Yukica (Dartmouth)

# Creating an Offensive Advantage with the Perimeter Attack Offense

What is the philosophy of your offensive system? It doesn't really matter whether you discuss answers to that question with junior high, high school, collegiate, or pro coaches—sooner or later the topic focuses on how the defensive perimeter is attacked. Some coaches finesse the corner, some option it, some block it, others pass against it; but regardless, each coach generally has his pet way to get to the outside. What he wants to know is how others might attack the perimeter, and how defenses defend it.

In fact, the desire to prevent offenses from getting outside is a basic philosophy of most defensive schemes. We define the perimeter of the defense as that area between the primary contain man and the closest forcing defender from the inside-out. How that "running lane" or defensive perimeter is attacked is the key function of this book.

Having coached at the high school level, and coaching now in college, the main difference between the two levels is not the intricacies of the X's and O's, but recruiting. The college coach is normally given the opportunity to "find" the type of personnel that will fit best into his particular offensive and defensive schemes. The high school coach is generally forced to make do with the material that just happens to be at his school. The better coaches, regardless of the level at which they compete, are the ones who can properly evaluate the strengths and weaknesses of their personnel, as well as that of their opponents, and strategically create an offensive or defensive advantage whereby personnel strengths are magnified and weaknesses are screened.

It is for these coaches that *The Perimeter Attack Offense: Key to Winning Football* has been written. While the heart of the offense and this book is the actual attack on the corner, no offense can be totally sound by just exploiting the perimeter. A complete analysis of the offense takes place here: the base running plays are complemented by companion misdirection and play action plays, as well as the major schemes to attack the defensive interior and off-tackle on the ground, and the short, intermediate, and deep zones in the air. This book does *not* assume that the coach has a stable of studs, but analyzes enough intricacies of the offense to make it adaptable, whether in whole, or in part, to the talents of the available personnel. It has been broken down in a sequential chapter by chapter order, to make the most sense and to provide the most advantage to the reader.

I know that there are coaches who firmly believe that the game of football has not changed over the last 25 years. To them, the game will always be won by the team who makes the fewest mistakes, and who does the best job of blocking, tackling, and running—period! There isn't a coach worth his salt in this country, at any level, who does not believe that excellence of execution (and decent personnel) wins football games. This is a basic philosophy of the Perimeter Attack Offense. However, to say that the game hasn't changed simply isn't true. There has been a much greater emphasis on design, technique, detail, and organization, and it seems to increase from year to year. While the heart of the game hasn't changed, certainly the design and detail, within which systems execute, have.

I have had the opportunity to coach both offense and defense. While I know that offensive and defensive coaching specialists exist, the great offensive minds are great because they thoroughly understand defensive philosophies, concepts, and techniques. The same, of course, is true of a great defensive mind in his understanding of offense.

I have always thought defensively when preparing my own offensive systems and game plans. While I can't help but be somewhat biased, the beauty of this book and this offense for me has been the fact that, when I look at it as a defensive coach at the college level now, the offense seems that much more sound and truly effective as a bonafide attack on any defense. As potent as it was as a high school offense, it will one day be just as convincing a weapon at the college level.

   As you read this book, I challenge you to think in terms of a defensive coach forced to stop it. It is truly in that context where the effectiveness of the system stands tall and takes root. From the ideas presented, see if you can create an *offensive advantage.*

                                                                J.M.

# Table of Contents

Chapter 12: Polishing Off the Perimeter Attack ...........229

# 1

# Organizing the Perimeter Attack

While the heart of this book lies in Chapters Two through Twelve, this chapter explains those concepts that will help in understanding how the *Perimeter Attack Offense* is organized.

The philosophy of the offense is broken down into play series, where each series has its base play or plays, counters and misdirections off those plays, and play action passes coming off certain segments of the running game, just as screens and draws come off the heart of the dropback and sprint out passing schemes.

While most coaches would consider the offense balanced, there has not been an effort to achieve a 50-50 run-pass ratio. Rather, both the run and pass exist as supplements to each other. They feed off each other and enhance each other.

The blood and guts of the Perimeter Attack Offense is its attack on the defensive perimeter. Each chapter gives a step-by-step look at that attack and at all of its variations. Most plays are broken down into the following:

- *Play objective:* This explains exactly what the purpose and the function of the play is, and how it fits in with the rest of the series.

- *Position responsibilities:* This goes into detail on the precise job that each player is to execute for each play, regardless of the situation in which the play is called and against what defense the play is to be run.

- *Blocking pattern:* This is really a simplified version for each position responsibility. It deals with whomever is to be blocked, and exactly what each man's job is for each of the plays versus *any* defense of variation. It is designed specifically for this offense. Each play has its own blocking pattern, and while it may seem a bit difficult at first glance, it will lead to eliminating indecision, increasing overall offensive position coordination, and reducing errors. A player does not have to understand total defensive concepts, but just what can happen in his area, and be able to communicate that recognition with his teammates. Each blocking pattern is to be memorized and thoroughly understood.

- *Play look and variation:* For clarity, the base plays and any major variations are diagrammed and explained.

- *Unique fundamentals:* Regardless of the philosophies, concepts, or schemes illustrated in this book, the heart of my philosophy is excellence of execution. Without it, even the best offensive machine would be ineffective, or would operate well below top efficiency. However, the purpose of this book is *not* to get into a discussion of fundamentals, unless the fundamentals are a little different and an explanation is necessary for proper understanding.

- *Coaching note:* Where appropriate, Coach's Notes are listed for clarity or emphasis.

- *Supporting statistics:* For some of the plays, specific stats have been kept since the play has been used. These stats are implemented to show the effectiveness of the play in certain areas and under different conditions. Keep in mind that I was a Head High School Coach at two very different schools. The one thing both schools had in common, however, was that both programs had been very much down and required major rebuilding situations. The first was a small private school; the second was a large public school.

This chapter is designed to give the preliminaries of the overall Perimeter Attack Offense, to demonstrate its "nonfundamental" basics and organization.

## PERIMETER ATTACK PERSONNEL

One of the biggest differences I find between coaching high school and college is recruiting. Many colleges will go after that type of athlete who best fits into the type of player mold that coaches look for in running a specific type of offense. Such a luxury does not generally exist at the high school level. A coach, at that level, can either force a player to fit into a certain type of mold to fit his offensive system, or else adapt that system to emphasize the strengths and to screen the weaknesses of his personnel. The better coaches, at *any* level, know that the better the use they make of their personnel will be to their advantage in the long run.

There is not a sane coach in the country who does not prefer to have the best possible players that he can get. There is a direct correlation between success and having great players. However, there are coaches who have great players, but don't win with them. There are also coaches who have poor talent, but make them competitive; have players of average talent, but make them good; and win championships with good talent and better.

### Position Goals

Like most football programs, we use our share of motivational devices for our team. We always have goals for our offense, defense, kicking units, overall team, in the short range, in the long range, etc. However, in our discussion of personnel and individual positions, we always preach and coach the idea of each player becoming the best he can at his position. While no individual goal is ever more important than anything discussed for the team or program in general, we have statements placed on plywood in the locker room about the great lineman, back, receiver, and quarterback (QB). These thoughts also appear in our Offensive Playbook.

When you take a close look at the thoughts mentioned, the old reliable traits such as *desire, pride, determination,* and *attitude* are the underlying concepts. Each of these statements follows. Keep in mind that these are used as motivational devices and reminders for our players, and should be thought of in that vein now.

### The great lineman

Every good lineman is able to do his job at the point of attack (POA). The great lineman, however, is not only effective at the POA, but away from it as well. The great lineman makes good, hard, aggressive contact regardless of the POA. He not only hustles to get downfield but he makes a block downfield. The great lineman explodes like a caged animal on the snap, making super initial contact and quality follow-through. The great lineman never makes mental errors; he always knows his assignments, and he has football sense. He is always a hard worker, dedicated, and a team leader.

Most of all, every great lineman knows the game will be won or lost by the team who does the best job of controlling the line of scrimmage (LOS). A team that has linemen always striving for greatness will be in contention for team championships.

### The great back

The good back must be able to run, block, and catch. The great back becomes known as a true triple threat. He can win for his team when the ball is in his hands or when he is blocking for someone else. The great back runs both inside and outside with authority, speed, and power. He thinks and adjusts on the move, but most importantly, he has a burning, uncontrollable desire never to go down. When he is faked to, he makes the defense believe he has the ball, he blocks with a controlled abandonment, and he comes up with the big catch and runs through a team's passing attack. The great back makes plays succeed even when they shouldn't; even broken plays succeed if the great back has his say.

### The great receiver

The good receiver can catch the ball; otherwise, he wouldn't be playing that position. The great receiver, however, catches balls other receivers can't even get to. He catches the ball in a crowd and in the clutch, and he never hears footsteps. The great receiver always knows how to get open, where he should be, and how to get there. A football seems to have an attraction for the great receiver. Even the best of defensive backs can't tell if he is a primary target in a particular pattern, for the great receiver always runs his routes at top speed.

The great receiver is always a top blocker. Whether on the LOS or downfield, whether at the POA or away from it, the great receiver proves he is to be respected for his physical toughness and blocking ability, just as much as his great hands.

### The great quarterback

First and foremost, the great quarterback is always a team man and a leader, both on and off the field. He has a super attitude and is a very dedicated, committed worker. If he makes an error, he never feels sorry for himself, for he is the first one to bounce back and make up for his mistake or that of a teammate. He always puts the welfare of the team ahead of his own. He knows the difference between pain and injury, and he plays over pain.

He may not always be the best passer or runner, but the great QB is a fierce competitor who is always a winner. He makes things happen; one way or another, he gets the job done.

The wisest of quarterbacks also remembers one important thing; his best friends are his line, and he goes nowhere without congratulating them and giving them credit.

## HUDDLE

The entire philosophy of our offense, and indeed, our overall program, begins with something that is disciplined, sharp, and snappy. The quarterback (QB) faces the line of scrimmage (LOS). The team faces the QB with the strong guard (SG) calling the huddle. The SG aligns on the ball and 10 yards from it. To the SG's left are the center (C) and the strong back (StB). To the SG's right are the strong tackle (ST) and the strong end (StE). Directly behind the SG is the quick back (QkB). To his left are the quick tackle (QT) and the quick guard (QG). To his right are the slot back or the flanker (SB-Fl) and the quick end (QE).

_____ LOS

QE    SB    QkB    QT    QG

StE   ST    SG     C    StB

QB

## Huddle Call

When the QB is ready, he steps in front of the SG and signals "check." Whenever possible throughout the huddle call and cadence, words with one syllable are used. This enhances the sharp and snappy nature of the offense. In unison, the huddle signals "check" back to the QB, while the first line snaps forward placing their hands on their knees, and the back line folds their hands in front of them.

Just before the QB gives the first "check" command, he gives the down and distance. Once the team signals "check" back, the QB gives the formation, series, play, and snap count. The snap count is given twice. After it is given the first time, the C leaves the huddle so he is the first to line up. At the end of the second snap count, the QB signals "check" again. The huddle responds with another "check" as they clap their hands in unison, break the huddle, and *sprint* to their set position.

## Flip-Flop Alignments

As implied by the position names in the huddle, the entire offense, except for the C and the QB, do flip-flop with the formation. The main reason for this is that tremendous proficiency can be gained by a player when he concentrates on one job, since he generally will have less overall responsibilities.

## CADENCE

The cadence is to be Loud, Authoritative, and Crisp (LAC). It is also to be rhythmic.

## Basic Procedure

1. The QB checks the alignment and gets set. He will always look to the quick side first, then to the strong side.

2. Before the cadence begins, while everyone is still in the set position, if the QB is to give either a shift command or an automatic signal, he does so now.

3. On "set," the team *snaps* into their stances. Prior to this command, everyone except the C is in a two-point stance. On "set," the line goes to four-point stance, while the receivers and backs snap to a three-point stance.

Approximately one-third of the time the ball is snapped on "set." Over the years, going on a quick count has given us advantages; it helps eliminate defensive stemming altogether prior to the snap, and more importantly, it aids in our execution. When attacking the perimeter, when pass blocking, and when pulling, the first step that most of our linemen take is a lateral or drop-step. Being able to do this from a two-point stance aids in making that step as fast as possible, while still being able to see the entire defensive zone in a player's area.

The QB must remember that the entire unit must be set for a complete count before the ball can be snapped. If the set backs are to do any shifting, they do it now, unless a "shift" call has already been given.

4. "Check" follows "set." The ball is never snapped on "check." It is given to allow the line and the receivers time to make their calls, and to ensure that the team has been set a full count before the ball is snapped.

5. "Hut" follows "check." A "hut" is given in rhythmic fashion for each number given in the snap count. A pause exists between each "hut." The snap count is generally "one," but "two" and "three" will also be taken advantage of. We try to go on "two" in most normal third and less than five situations, but *not* in third and short.

## The Long Cadence

In certain situations, like fourth and less than five, an abnormally long cadence is used. Most of the time, if the defense hasn't gone offside by "five," the QB will call a time-out. Once in a while, we will run a play on "five," but only if we feel we can afford to give up the ball in that particular field position. We are especially conscious of doing this against overly-aggressive clubs and in the first half, when most teams don't use their share of time-outs, anyhow.

## Coaching Note

It is important to emphasize here that the cadence used on the perimeter attack, while it may not seem overly novel or innovative, is by no means taken for granted by either our staff or the offense. It is strategically used and coached to gain a specific advantage.

## Automatics

When and why a team uses an audible system is mainly a function of that team's philosophy and game plan. With the proper coordination between position communication and the blocking pattern, to automatic at the LOS is not that great a priority, since each blocking pattern is uniquely designed to handle adequately any defensive look it faces. However, as will become more evident later in the book, a most simple automatic system has proven to be a real plus in the overall scheme of the perimeter attack.

### "Auto"

When a QB calls a play in the huddle, 95 percent of the time that play will be run at the LOS. However, there are times when we know *what* we want called, but are not sure which side we should run it to, until we see where the defense aligns. These are also the times where it is best to call the actual play at the line. Examples of this are the *special series* (Chapter Eleven) and the *conversion series* (Chapter Twelve). Note that we do not automatic, as such, because the defense seems stacked to the play—the blocking pattern will handle that.

In the huddle, the word *"auto"* is given right after the formation. This alerts the team to the fact that prior to the "set" call being given at the LOS, the QB will call one number twice. That number will be the play. The entire team knows from the game plan what numbers represent which plays. When the QB wants to give a direction for a specific play, he names the play after he says "auto" in the huddle; for example, "auto-pitch." An even number at the LOS means the pitch will be run to the right, an odd number means to the left.

Sometimes, of course, "dummy" numbers are given at the LOS. The only law that we give the QB is to never give a dummy number when the snap count is on "set." We have had very few mistakes with this system.

### "Goose"

The QB may run this at any time. He simply pinches the leg of the C to whichever side he wants to go. As the QB exerts pressure up on the C's butt with his hands for the exchange, the C snaps the ball, and the C and the QB run a *sneak*. While the rest of the line is expected to block accordingly, once the "goose" is realized, no one on the field knows what's coming except the QB and the C.

The QB might run the "goose" anytime he sees that the defense is not respecting the middle, or as a complete element of surprise. To be truly effective, a quality perimeter attack must force the defense to defend the middle. Our QBs are coached to be aware of this.

## LINE COMMUNICATION

Line communication basically accomplishes two objectives. First, it describes what the defense looks like in a specific area; and second, it coordinates that defensive area with the play's blocking pattern. On each play, each lineman "calls" his immediate area, which spans the "on the line" and linebacker (LB) area from the near shoulder of the positions lined up to his left and right. When a defender is considered to be head up, he is called "on." If the defender is to the offensive player's inside, "in" is called; if outside of him, "out" is called. If defenders are both inside and outside, "double" is called.

Two common criticisms of most blocking rules are that they (1) tend to be too technical, and therefore, their interpretation and execution become somewhat confusing; and (2) they tend to be too general, and therefore, in order to find the best way to block a specific defense, exceptions have to be made.

The way the blocking patterns for the perimeter attack is set up, the above problems are eliminated. Each offensive play within a series has both a hole number for a point of attack (POA) and a play objective. While each POA begins with a specific hole, the blocking pattern may vary that POA based on what the offensive players see in their immediate area.

Once these concepts are understood, the ability to execute the blocking pattern lies with the player's ability to recognize what has to be done in his immediate area to accomplish both the execution of the blocking pattern and the play objective. This means that *whether or not a defender is considered "in," "on," "out," or "double" is technically determined by the linemen at their own discretion as guided by the blocking pattern and play objective.*

## Coach's Note

I know this may seem complicated, but once it is understood, it is a most functional weapon. Each play's blocking pattern, play objective, and line call will hold up as a quality way to attack *any* defense. By no stretch of the imagination do the players have to be honor students to understand and execute these principles. In fact, it is precisely these principles that *greatly* enhance execution.

Anything that can't be coached without breeding some hesitation or indecision in its execution is *not* a part of the Perimeter Attack Offense.

## FORMATIONS

The blocking patterns and the play designs for the perimeter attack are set up to take advantage of multiple formation looks. Over the years, four basic formations have been used: *slot, pro, power,* and *special.* From the slot and pro, four different backfield sets have been used: *split, strong, quick,* and *I.*

The *slot* is the most used formation, and will be the one most used for illustration purposes in this book. The slot can be used to the right or left. Alignment for the set backs is generally predetermined going into each game. Consequently, it is not always necessary to call both for formation and backfield set in the huddle. The *pro,* like the slot, can also be used to the right or left. The strong back always takes a normal fullback type of alignment, while the quick back aligns to the slot or pro back in a strong set, away from the slot or pro back in a weak set, and in a normal tailback set in the I.

While the *power* can also be called to the left or right, the backfield remains stable and takes on a wishbone type of look. The quick back aligns to the quick end and the slot or pro back aligns opposite the quick back.

The *special* formation is unique and will be handled in Chapter Eleven.

Diagram 1-1 shows slot left with split backs, while Diagram 1-2 illustrates slot right with a quick look. Diagram 1-3 shows a pro left with quick backs, and Diagram 1-4 is a pro right with an I. Power right is illustrated in Diagram 1-5.

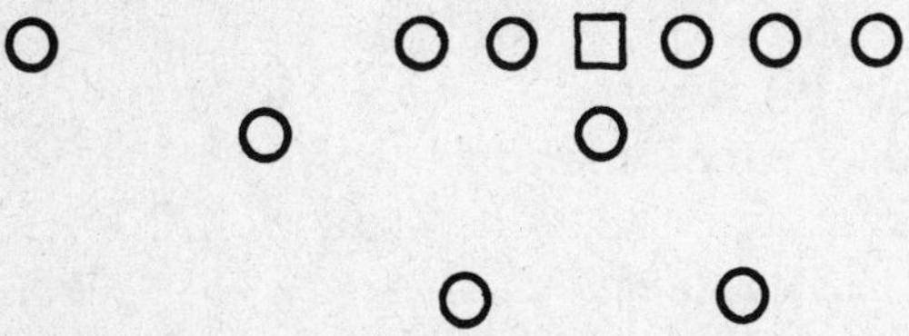

DIAGRAM 1-1

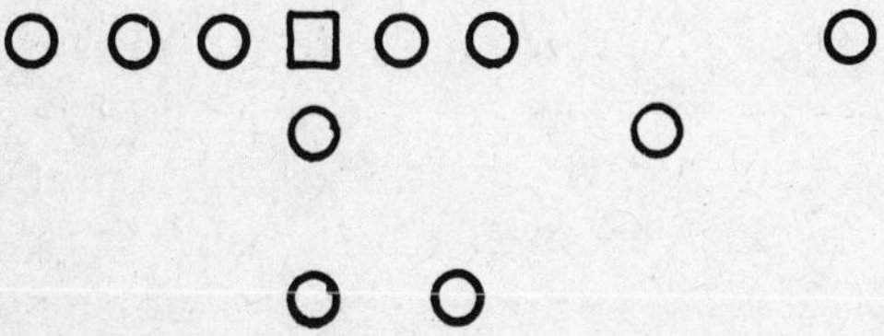

DIAGRAM 1-2

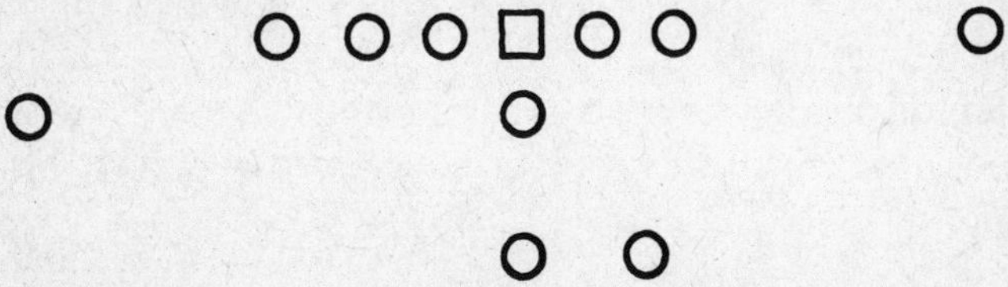

DIAGRAM 1-3

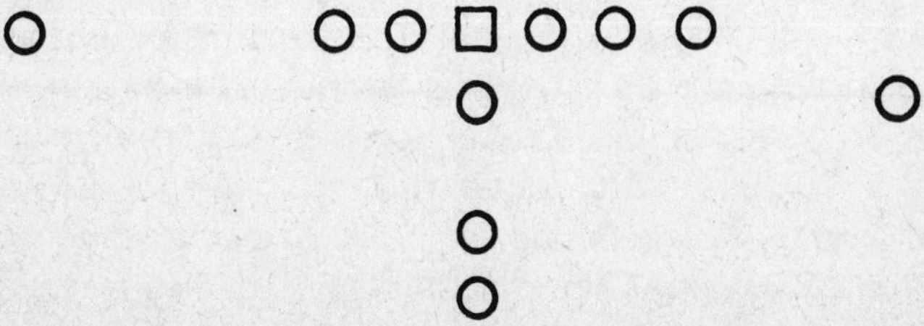

DIAGRAM 1-4

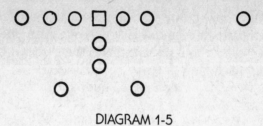

DIAGRAM 1-5

## Line Splits

The actual splits of the line will vary from play to play and series to series. Both the slot and the pro formations employ a minimum-maximum split philosophy. A minimum split would be one foot, a maximum would be three feet. In general, when the play is being run inside, we prefer a maximum split, thereby enhancing the room the runner has to work with as he hits the POA. When going outside, a minimum split is preferred. This generally tightens the defense without cutting down on the speed with which we get to the perimeter.

The side of the line that the play is not going to must vary its split; the side that the play is going to must reverse its tendency on occasion; that is, keep maximum splits on an outside play, and minimum splits on an inside. Each lineman is responsible for his own split, as long as his split doesn't have an adverse effect on his teammate's ability to carry out his blocking pattern. In this way enough variance is built into the system to make it effective without giving too much away to the defense.

In a power formation, the splits are constant; two feet between the center and guards, and three feet between the guards and tackles.

## Positioning of the Set Backs and Receivers

While the basic alignment of the backs and receivers has already been discussed, the *exact* depth and width of the backs and the *exact* split of the receivers, is a function of the play objective, and the ability of the personnel involved when coordinated with the rest of the teammates. As an example, a really quick back may, in general, have to take a deeper alignment for an inside play, and one that is not so wide on an outside play. His alignment is a function of the timing between himself, the QB, and anyone else who has a responsibility that may affect what his starting point is on a play.

The split of the strong end may be anywhere from 1 to 4 yards. The slot may be anywhere from 1 through 6 yards. The pro back can go from 3 through 12 yards on his alignment, as can the quick end. This is also a function of the play objective. In general, however, the alignment of the slot back and the quick end in the slot formation will be 3 yards from the tackle and the slot, respectively. In the pro formation, the pro back and the quick end will generally take a 6-yard split, and in the power formation, the quick end will do the same.

One again, it is important to keep in mind that these splits must vary from onside to offside, and to reverse tendencies on occasion.

## Coach's Note

In the beginning, when first learning the position responsibilities and the blocking patterns, there may be some confusion in the splits that a particular player should take. Here's where it is imperative that the coach often question and quiz his players as to *why* they take a certain alignment, as dictated by series and play objectives, and by his own blocking patterns. Patience for the coach is certainly a virtue here, for once the confusion is eliminated, the total understanding of his specific job that each player develops becomes a tremendous advantage later on.

## Motion

This designates a normal motion movement by the slot or pro back. In the huddle, it is called "mo," and generally begins at the LOS on the QB's nod.

## Fly

This is the same as "mo," except it designates that one of the set backs will go into motion. In the huddle, it is called "fly," and once again, begins at the LOS by the QB's nod. The term "mo" or "fly" is given after the play is called in the huddle.

### Shift

When the word "shift" precedes the formation given in the huddle, the offense breaks the huddle and comes out in the opposite side formation than what was called. Before the actual cadence begins, the command "shift" is given at the LOS. The offense then shifts to the called formation. The QB waits a full count, and then begins the normal cadence.

### Effectiveness of Mo—Fly—Shift

Which of these concepts we employ going into a game is really a function of that week's game plan. With very little extra preparation, it has proven quite effective against teams who stem (change their alignment prior to our snap), monster to a particular side, or flip-flop personnel.

However, as part of our philosophy, it is a must that we have our actual execution and technique down before taking advantage or "mo," "fly," or "shift." If using any of these has any negative effect on our execution, they are not used.

### Shotgun

When "shotgun" is added at the end of a play called in the huddle, the QB either aligns in or shifts to a shotgun alignment 5 yards behind the center. This is generally used against teams with vicious pass rushes on passing downs. The primary disadvantage to it is that it virtually eliminates our running game repertoire, as well as the setback draw, which is a big part of our passing game. The advantage to it is that it almost gets our QB set to throw prior to the snap, and makes the reads of his keys a little easier.

## NUMBERING SYSTEM

Solely for the purpose of being able to communicate quickly and clearly in the huddle, all of our formations, series, plays, and holes are numbered. The following makes up that numbering system; all even numbers are to the right.

## Hole Numbers

8: Between the C and the right guard (RG). Note that whether or not the RG is the SG or the QG is a function of the formation called.

6: Between the RG and the RT.

4: Between the RT and the receiver.

2: Outside the StE or the SB's normal alignment.

7: Between the C and the LG.

5: Between the LG and the LT.

3: Between the LT and the receiver.

1: Outside the StE or the SB's normal alignment.

## Formations

When each play is called in the huddle, a three-digit number is given; the first digit designates the formation. Once again, odd numbers mean the formation goes to the left, and even means to the right.

100(200): Slot left (slot right).

300(400): Pro left (pro right).

500(600): Power left (power right). Whether the power is left or right is determined by the QE.

SPECIAL: No numbers are used here, just words.

## Series

One of the three-digit number given in the huddle, the second digit designates the play series. There is no need to designate left or right.

10: Sneak Series

20: Pitch Series (Includes Ride and Pitch Counter Series)

30: Lead Series

40: Dive Series

50: Power Series

60: Option Series

70: I Series

90: Air Series

SPECIAL: No numbers used here.

## Play Calls

The last digit of the three-digit number called in the huddle designates the play itself. Even-numbered plays are run to the right and odd to the left. It is important to note, however, that the play itself is not *always* the exact hole for the POA. The POA may change within a play dependent upon the coordination of the defensive recognition calls made by the offensive players and the blocking pattern. In general, though, the play numbers used are the hole numbers those plays are designed to attack. The following are those plays within each series.

*1. Sneak series (teens)*

SNEAK LEFT: 17

SNEAK RIGHT: 18. Remember, odd numbers designate the play is run to the left and even to the right.

*2. Pitch series (twenties)*

Pitch: 21 (22)

Pitch Pass: 21 (22) Pass

Pitch Read: 21 (22) Read

Pitch Trailer: 21 (22) Trailer

Pitch Screen: 21 (22) Screen

Ride: 23 (24)

Ride Pass: 23 (24) Pass

Ride Charge: 23 (24) Charge

Reverse: 25 (26)

Reverse Pass: 25 (26) Pass

Pitch Trap: 27 (28)
Pitch Trap Boot: 27 (28) Boot

*3. Lead series (thirties)*

Lead: 35 (36)
Lead Pass: 35 (36) Pass
Lead Scissors: 33 (34)
Lead Boot: 35 (36) Boot
Lead Boot Pass: 35 (36) Boot Pass
Lead Around: 35 (36) Around

*4. Dive series (forties)*

Dive: 45 (46)
Dive Keeper: 41 (42)
Dive Pop Pass: 45 (46) Pop

*5. Power series (fifties)*

Power: 55 (56)
Power Pass: 55 (56) Pass
Power Pitch: 51 (52)

*6. Option series (sixties)*

Option: 61 (62)
Option Pass: 61 (62) Pass
Ride Option: 63 (64)

*7. I series (seventies)*

Isotak: 73 (74)
Isotak Charge: 73 (74) Charge
Isotak Pass: 73 (74) Pass
Isotak Sprint: 73 (74) Sprint
Isolation-Ice: 75 (76)
Ice Dive: 77 (78)

Ice Lead: 75 (76) Lead

I Options: 71 (72)

*8. Air option series (nineties)*

Air Option: 91 (92)

Air Option Screen: 93 (94)

*9. Special series*

This entire series, from formation to play to direction, employs words only.

Sneak Left (Right)

Lead (can be run to the strong side only when the ball is on
    the hash)

Pitch Left (Right)

Pitch Pass Left (Right)

Screen Left (Right)

## Examples of Play Calls

The following are simple examples of play calls made in the huddle with their literal meaning explained:

a. 121: Slot left, pitch left.

b. Shift 236: Begin in a slot left, shift to a slot right, lead right.

c. 124 mo: Slot left with SB motion, ride right.

d. 446 fly: Pro right with strong back in motion, dive right.

e. 374: Pro left, Isotak right.

f. 191 shotgun: Slot left, QB shotgun, air option left.

g. 555: Power formation left, power left.

h. Special, pitch right: Special, pitch right.

## THE SNEAK

While the heart of this book is the attack on the perimeter, the first play we teach each year is the *sneak.* The sneak is a weapon that is far too often taken for granted. It can be used most effectively against a defense. It is a play that we practice every day to perfection. The beauty of it is that this whole concept of perfection can be more easily reached in the sneak than in any other play. The way the blocking pattern is set up, it can effectively be run against any defense with only four players actively involved in the play: the C, both Gs, and the QB.

## Play Objective

In reality, there are two plays in this series—the sneak itself and the *goose automatic*. The sneak can be considered a quick hitter that can be used to take advantage of defenses who give the offense a soft middle. It can also be used effectively against teams that stunt to the outside a lot. In this way, it becomes an element of surprise.

In short yardage situations, the sneak functions as a sure way to pick up necessary yards. It does not, however, hit a specific POA. The QB will attack daylight by properly reading his keys as defined in the blocking pattern.

If the sneak is successful at surprising the defense and the QB gets past the linebackers, there could be a big gain, especially since there will be much downfield blocking.

## Position Responsibilities

### Line

CENTER: He blocks anyone aligned head up as in an odd defensive set. If no one is there, he blocks anyone aligned in his playside gap who is on the LOS; and finally, if no one is there, he blocks the near LB. If both guards give a double-gap call, he crosses with the onside guard.

GUARDS: They block the inside gap first. If no one is there, they block anyone considered head up. If no one is there, they use a *slide* technique to get to the LB. The slide technique is nothing more than the guard stepping with his inside foot straight upfield. He keeps his shoulders square to the goal line, never allowing a defender aligned on his outside shoulder to cross his face. This gives the QB just enough time to get past any pinching defensive lineman who has aligned outside of the guards, without actually having to block that defender.

TACKLES: Both tackles ignore anyone to their inside. They use a *slide* technique on anyone aligned head up or outside. If a LB comes near their path, they block him; otherwise, they get downfield to the middle third.

## Backfield

QUARTERBACK: He takes one short step back with the foot to the direction in which the play is being run. This is much like the step that an I tailback takes for balance and extra power. Prior to taking this step, he reads the keys to determine which seam will be the most beneficial to attack.

Versus an odd defensive set, he reads the nose guard. If he takes a slide after the snap, he hits the opposite hole. If he doesn't, he goes to the onside called in the huddle, since this will be the breast that the center will attack. If the nose is offset to one side of the center, the other seam is attacked.

Versus any other gap or even defensive set, he attacks the first vacant seam between the guards. If both are occupied, he attacks the first vacant seam between the tackles, hugging the outside hip of the onside guard. When both seams are vacant, he attacks the onside seam first. When all four seams are occupied, the center and the onside guard will cross, so he attacks directly up the spinal column of the onside guard's alignment.

SET BACK: Both flare to fake the release of the pitch.

## Receivers

All three receivers get downfield and pick up the first defenders that show from the outside third toward the middle.

# The Blocking Pattern

## Line

C: On, onside gap on the LOS, backside gap on the LOS, near LB. Crosses with the onside gap versus quadruple gaps.

Gs: Gap, on, slide. If onside, cross with the C versus quadruple gaps.

Ts: Slide.

*Backfield*

QB: Versus odd set—opposite the movement or alignment of the nose. Versus any other set—attacks first vacant seam between the tackles. Goes inside first. Splits the onside G's butt versus quadruple gaps.

SET BACKS: Flare.

*Receivers*

All downfield.

## Play Look and Variations

In Diagrams 1-6, 1-7, and 1-8, note the actual POA the QB will hit as determined by both the blocking pattern and defensive set. All three diagrams illustrate a *sneak left*. In Diagram 1-6, the nose is offset and the QB will hit the offside C-G seam as his POA. In Diagram 1-7, both C-G seams are filled, so the QB will hit the G-T seam to the left. In Diagram 1-8, there will be a quadruple gap called ("double" gaps called by both guards). Consequently, the QB's POA is the butt of the onside guard, since the onside guard and the center will cross.

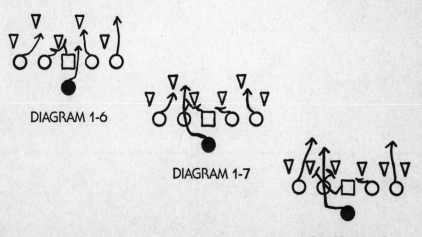

DIAGRAM 1-6

DIAGRAM 1-7

DIAGRAM 1-8

# 2

# A Unique Look at the Quick Pitch

The *quick pitch* in the perimeter game takes on new life in terms of its emphasis and how it is run. A complete analytical look is done in this chapter as it deals with the play objective, responsibilities, and techniques.

## PLAY OBJECTIVE: QUICK PITCH

Most times, the key to the success of a play series is the proper execution of the base play, upon which that play series is based. The pitch is geared at attacking the perimeter of the defense, and it is important that the offense becomes known for the pitch. With continued practice and proper execution, the pitch becomes almost unstoppable, and of course, there is a reason for this. Refer to Diagrams 2-14 and 2-15 to get a basic feel for the play.

### Eight to Six Offensive to Defensive Ratio

In Diagrams 2-1, 2-2, and 2-3, a specific offense to defense ratio is illustrated. On the snap of the ball, a specific offensive advantage is gained when the pitch is run properly, especially in a quick backfield set.

In Diagram 2-1 the offense is attacking a base 5-2 Oklahoma defensive set with a straight four-deep secondary. Once the ball is snapped, the initial action of the C, QB, and FB takes them to the onside of the midline. Those three, plus the G, T, slot, SE, and QkB who are already aligned onside, give the offense eight men who are already in motion to the onside of the midline with specific responsibilities and assignments. If you extend the midline through the defensive alignment and assume that the middle guard (MG) reacts to the C's head, there are only six defensive people to the onside at the initial snap of the ball. Most defensive coaches would agree that the five backside defenders are either too far away from the immediate point of attack or have counter, bootleg, or throwback responsibilities that they must first check for before frontside pursuit takes place.

Even when the front goes to a stack overshift and prerotates the secondary to offensive strength, there is still an eight to seven advantage in personnel for the offense. See Diagram 2-2.

In the split-4 even set in Diagram 2-3, the defense still can get only six men to the onside, especially since that offside LB normally has counter responsibility first, and "pursuit lag" second.

If the offense has a consistent number advantage over the defense, how then can the pitch be stopped? When the play is executed properly, the defense is forced to "cheat" or to overcom-

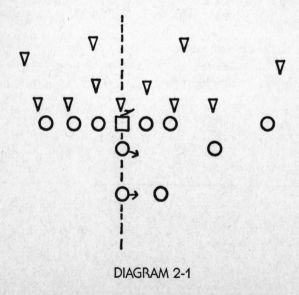

DIAGRAM 2-1

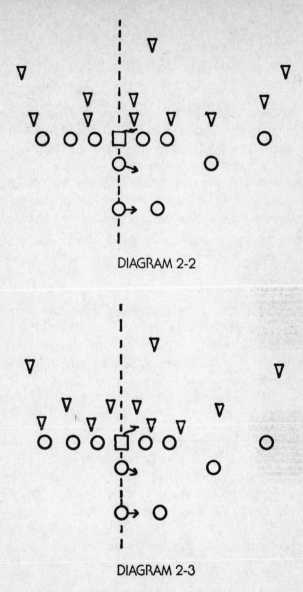

DIAGRAM 2-2

DIAGRAM 2-3

pensate to the corner in order to equalize what had been a disadvantage. While it is exactly this overcompensation by the defense that may take the pitch away, it is also that compensation that opens the rest of the series and can turn those plays into game breakers.

## POSITION RESPONSIBILITIES

### Line

ONSIDE TACKLE: Pulls behind the receiver and attacks the outside breast of the first man to show on the corner outside the widest receiver's block. If no one appears immediately, he looks to the inside for invert support and containment on the corner.

If containment occurs quickly and on the line of scrimmage, he still continues to run at the outside, thereby forcing the contain man to overcompensate.

ONSIDE GUARD: Takes a lateral step to the onside checking for any penetration to frontside gap from a down man or linebacker. He must be prepared for penetration from any direction.

If there is no immediate pressure, he does not hesitate. He explodes off his frontside foot at a perpendicular to the line of scrimmage, attacking the outside hip of the first man to show either on the line of scrimmage or on a pursuit angle to the ball.

If no pressure shows, he gets to the track, never letting an opponent cross his face while on route.

CENTER: Same as the onside guard.

OFFSIDE GUARD: Pulls behind the center and blocks the first odd shirt to show. He starts to penetrate the line of scrimmage once past the center, but does not stay parallel to the line. If there is no one to effectively block early, he turns upfield and gets to the track as soon as possible, never allowing an opponent to cross his face. The first block may take place as soon as the neutral zone is cleared.

### Receivers

QUICK END:

*If onside:* Blocks the first man to the inside on or off the line of scrimmage, but does not block anyone on the line of scrimmage who is aligned inside the slot back.

If there is no immediate danger to the inside, the game plan may dictate to release downfield to attack the first defensive back who shows on the corner as a primary contain man. Players must always be most conscious of all crackback blocking rules.

*If offside:* Attacks the frontside breast of the man responsible for covering the backside deep third or deep half area. He will normally be the last line of defense on a breakaway. The block on him may mean the score. Or, he takes a three-step release off the line of scrimmage beginning with the outside foot, and then drives off that same outside foot back to the line of scrimmage to set up a fake screen. This is generally determined by the game plan.

SLOT BACK:

*If onside:* Blocks the first man to his inside that can affect the tackle on his pull or hurt the pitch itself by the quarterback. This opponent can be on or off the line of scrimmage. If no one is in the immediate vicinity to the slot's inside, he blocks the first man to show, beginning from an opponent who is head up, and then moves to the first man to the outside. An outside gap alignment by the defense would normally result in a double-team with the quick end.

*If offside:* Attacks the man in the middle deep third or onside deep half area if the quick end has backside third or half responsibility. He attacks the opponent in the backside third or half if the quick end is faking screen.

*If in motion to onside:* Goes into motion on the quarterback's nod; the ball will be snapped as the slot reaches the onside tackle's position. The slot back attacks the outside breast of the first man to show on the corner outside the strong end's block, but does not bypass an opposite-colored jersey should "leakage" take place.

*If in motion to offside:* The same motion routine and snap count should be executed as to the onside, but he should either turn upfield inside the strong end and attack the man in the deep third, or the half, if the strong end is faking screen. If the strong end is attacking deep third or half, he continues on motion track until the normal strong end position is reached and pivots back to the quarterback for screen.

STRONG END:

*If onside:* Executes the exact same job as the slot back when the slot is onside, but of course, there will be no double-team with the quick end, and the strong end will never go in motion.

*If offside:* Executes the exact same responsibility as the quick end, depending on the game plan.

## Backfield

QUARTERBACK: Pushes hard off the back foot while opening it 35 degrees; shuffles and makes pitch in one motion using the belt of the ballcarrier as the target point for the pitch; follows through.

QUICKBACK:

*If onside:* Opens release parallel to the line of scrimmage at top speed, always being prepared for the bad pitch. Once the pitch is caught, he rides the outside hip of the pulling tackle in an effort to get outside. He reads the tackle's block as he attacks the outside breast of the contain support on the corner. If the defender crosses the tackle's face, he cuts to the inside hip of the T tackle on a break perpendicular to the line of scrimmage.

*If offside:* He will open step as if to follow the pitch, then attack center-guard seam to the onside as if getting the ball for the *pitch trap.* If not tackled, he gets to track.

STRONG BACK: Exactly the same as the quick back.

## THE BLOCKING PATTERN

While the play position responsibilities give a detailed explanation of each player's exact responsibility, the blocking pattern is offered as a simple key guide to aid each player in understanding his responsibilities. Each player is expected to know verbatim his blocking pattern for each play, and to be able to explain it. We have found that the blocking pattern aids our players in eliminating indecision, increasing line coordination without hesitation, and reducing errors.

## Line

ONSIDE TACKLE: Pulls to outside breast of containment.

ONSIDE GUARD: Onside area run.

CENTER: Onside area run.

OFFSIDE GUARD: Pulls to set up counter.

OFFSIDE TACKLE: Track.

## Receivers

QUICK END: Inside, on, outside if onside, downfield or screen if offside.

SLOT BACK: Inside, on, outside if onside, downfield if offside.

SLOT BACK MOTION: Outside breast of containment if onside, downfield or screen if offside.

STRONG END: Inside, on, outside if onside, downfield or screen if offside.

## Backfield

QUARTERBACK: Pitch.

QUICKBACK: Opens parallel and attacks outside with tackle if onside. Fakes pitch traps if offside.

STRONG BACK: Same as quick back.

## THE RECEIVER DEFENSIVE RECOGNITION

It is imperative that the receivers (quick end, slot back, strong end) work together without hesitation. Each must be conscious of and be able to handle the type of adjustments that the defense makes to handle the corner game. Our receivers and the entire corner scheme we run tend to become a major source of aggravation for defenses in terms of their preparation. Consequently, numerous adjustments will be shown during the course of the season, and even during a game. The receivers must be prepared for each of these adjustments. Thus, the following recognitions are critical:

Diagram 2-4:    IN
Diagram 2-5:    ON
Diagram 2-6:    OUT
Diagram 2-7:    LOAD
Diagram 2-8:    STACK ON
Diagram 2-9:    STACK OUT
Diagram 2-10:   LOAD IN
Diagram 2-11:   LOAD OUT
Diagram 2-12:   SPLIT
Diagram 2-13:   SPLIT STACK

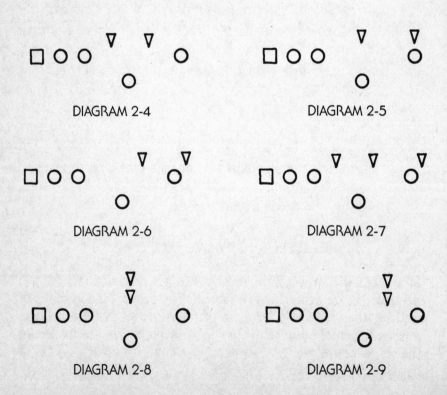

DIAGRAM 2-4                          DIAGRAM 2-5

DIAGRAM 2-6                          DIAGRAM 2-7

DIAGRAM 2-8                          DIAGRAM 2-9

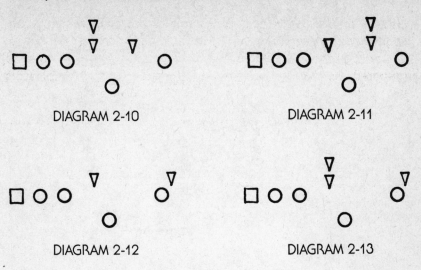

DIAGRAM 2-10                    DIAGRAM 2-11

DIAGRAM 2-12                    DIAGRAM 2-13

## Note One

Communication here is absolutely necessary among the receivers and sometimes between them and the tackles.

## Note Two

As mentioned earlier, in order to consistently stop the pitch, defenses cheat or overcompensate. Numerous adjustments are made on the corner in an effort to stop it. During the years that we have run this pitch, we have seen each of the above recognitions to our receiver alignment.

## BASE PLAY VARIATIONS AND LOOKS

Diagram 2-14 shows the pitch begin run from a slot right with a quick backfield set to the right side (222 would be the normal numbering system called in the huddle). It is being run against a base Oklahoma front with a straight four-deep secondary. If the defensive corner winds up crossing the pulling T's face, the QkB will cut to the inside hip of the T. Should the DE cause any problems on the corner, the SB and the QE can double-team him. It is also very important to note that should the onside DT penetrate hard in an effort to knock the pitch down, he will not be a problem.

This is due to the velocity and angle of the pitch, which will be explained in detail shortly.

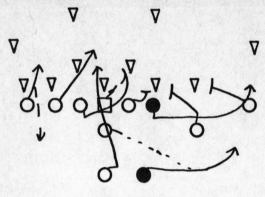

DIAGRAM 2-14

Diagram 2-15 shows a slot left, pitch left (121) against a split-4 defensive set. Assuming the SB feels that the DE can affect the play, he will seal him after stepping at the outside LB. This causes the QE to block the LB. If the SB doesn't feel the DE will affect the play, he will block the SB along with the QE on a double-team (Diagram 2-16). However, if the onside defensive corner comes up fast because of the down block by the QE, there are two variations in blocking that may take place. First, assuming the SB can handle the outside LB, the SB will take him, and the QE will run the corner off (Diagram 2-17). Second, the QE can seal the outside LB and the SB can pull behind the QE to the corner; the onside T, who

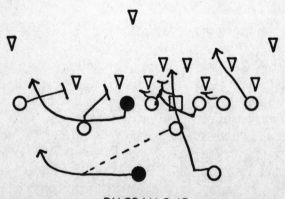

DIAGRAM 2-15

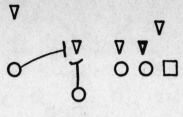

DIAGRAM 2-16

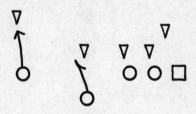

DIAGRAM 2-17

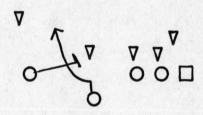

DIAGRAM 2-18

generally pulls, will block the onside area. This second variation in the blocking scheme is called "switch," and it is called by the SB at the LOS (Diagram 2-18). Note also that the backside middle LB in Diagram 2-15 is expected to hold for a count due to the pitch trap fake.

In Diagram 2-19, motion is used in a pro set with quick backs in an attack against an overshifted fifty look. We will assume that the secondary has adjusted to the motion effect and will invert support the playside corner. As the T pulls, if no one from the outside shows immediately as he turns the corner, he is to look inside for the invert support. The play is "322 mo." Note also that the QE's split should be about 6 yards. If he has trouble sealing the DE, the pro back can do it and the QE can attack the outside third (Diagram 2-20).

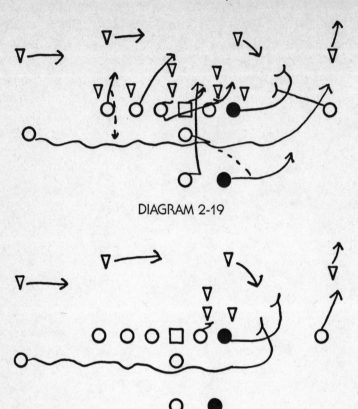

DIAGRAM 2-19

DIAGRAM 2-20

It should be obvious by now that there are a number of blocking variations that can take place on the corner. The receivers call their areas as described in the section on their recognition. Those calls, *plus* an evaluation of the opponents' personnel via for that week's scouting report, *plus* a thorough understanding of the blocking pattern, will determine exactly how the corner will be blocked in a particular week.

## THE ONSIDE DEFENSIVE TACKLE AREA

Initially, many defensive coaches think that a normal defensive tackle can affect the pitch itself by a quick, hard charge. Such a defensive technique, however, has not proven sound. The following are the reasons for this:

1. *Velocity of the pitch.* The angle of the pitch plus the quickness with which the pitch gets from the quarterback to the running back makes the pitch an extremely quick play.

2. *Parallel route of the running back.* With his normal depth of 4 to 5 yards and from his position behind the offensive tackle, the back will open-step to a parallel release with the line of scrimmage. This keeps the angle of the pitch relatively deep behind the line of scrimmage. It is a critical coaching point to keep the release of the back parallel to the line. If the back bends toward the line of scrimmage too soon, it flattens the angle of the pitch, and this is certainly not desired.

3. *Onside area block of the onside guard plus the inside block of the receiver.* As explained in the blocking responsibilities earlier, the onside guard reaches up while the receiver seals inside. This greatly limits the charge that the defensive tackle can take to the ball. See Diagram 2-21.

DIAGRAM 2-21

This is the only area that the defensive tackle can charge through without being banged by either the guard or the receiver. It is, however, both the velocity and the angle of the pitch that has the ball past this "danger zone" before even the quickest of the defensive tackles can get there.

**Note**

In running the pitch like this for the last seven years, the pitch was interfered with once, and that was due to a poor pitch technique. It is technically sound not to block that defensive tackle zone.

## SPECIFIC COACHING NOTES

### 1. On Cadence

While the pitch can be executed from any formation on any snap count, the initial movement of most of the people involved in the play is of a lateral nature. Therefore, a quick count ("set") facilitates this movement because of the nature of the two-point set position the offense is already in. It is easier to move laterally from a two-point stance, and consequently enhance the quickness and, sometimes, the surprise of the pitch.

## 2. On Crackback

Few things hurt a good-looking drive the way a 15-yard penalty can. With all the crackback blocking done by the receivers in a perimeter attack series, major penalties can be given for blocking below the waist or for clipping. It is of the utmost importance that the receivers know and understand what is and isn't a penalty, and that they are conscious of the importance of proper and legal execution here.

## NEW FUNDAMENTALS INVOLVED

### Making the Pitch

The QB take a 35-degree open pivot, pushing as hard as he can off his back instep and keeping a low center of gravity. He should hold the ball laces out, perpendicular to the ground, and next to his belt buckle. Thumbs should be toward the front of the ball with the fingers to the other side next to the QB's belt buckle. He should shuffle hard and snap the ball out, rotating his hand outward and cutting through the target area, which is the area just ahead of the ballcarrier's belt buckle. He should follow through by keeping his body lean and by running through the target area.

### Receiving the Pitch

Since the man receiving the pitch will be doing so while running at top speed, it is especially important to emphasize proper pitch fundamentals.

The shoulders should be turned slightly to the QB with complete concentration focused on the ball. The eyes should be on the ball until it is into the "carrying pocket." Always expect a bad pitch, for if the ballcarrier expects it, he will have little trouble with it.

Before, during, and after the pitch is made, the HB will be running. Once the ball is received, he should "pocket" it quickly.

## Attacking the Outside Breast

This is such an important technique in our offense, it deserved its own section. This is a downfield block, whereby the blocker attacks the outside breast of the defender by trying to "bite the nipple" of his outside breast. By doing so, the blocker tries to force and to maintain outside leverage on the defender.

As long as this outside leverage exists, the runner will continue to attack the outside and should indeed be able to get to the outside. The only way to prevent the blocker from gaining outside leverage is if the defender overcompensates. Once the back reads that the defender crosses his blocker's face, the back will cut hard inside on a perpendicular to the line of scrimmage and hug the hips of the blocker, thereby avoiding the inside-out pursuit.

It is also important that there be no hesitation and that the attack be made at top speed.

While we would prefer that the runner ride the outside hip of the blocker at about a depth of 3 yards, this will vary with the play.

## OUR QUICK-PITCH STATISTICS

In the seven years we have run our pitch this way, the following statistics have been accumulated:

| AT SCHOOL I | | | | | | |
|---|---|---|---|---|---|---|
| SEASON | GAMES | NO. RUN | TOTAL YARDS | AVG. GAIN | NEG. YARDS NO. PLAYS | LOST FUMBLES |
| SEASON I (4-5-0) | 9 | 63 | 321 | 5.1 | 5 | 4 |
| SEASON II (5-3-1) | 9 | 51 | 316 | 6.2 | 1 | 1 |
| SEASON III (8-1-0) | 9 | 71 | 497 | 7.0 | 2 | 1 |
| SEASON IV (8-1-0) | 9 | 69 | 496 | 7.2 | 3 | 0 |
| AT SCHOOL II | | | | | | |
| SEASON I (1-8-1) | 10 | 81 | 381 | 4.7 | 7 | 0 |
| SEASON II (3-7-0) | 10 | 68 | 367 | 5.4 | 4 | 1 |
| SEASON III (6-4-1) | 11 | 77 | 462 | 6.0 | 5 | 0 |

The play has been a most effective, consistent gainer. Both high school programs began as serious rebuilding situations. The four fumbles that were lost off the pitch the first year were due primarily to the technique of the pitch itself, which was at that time executed as an underhand spiral. The flat pitch we have made since then is a much easier ball to handle.

# 3

## Developing an Effective
## Perimeter Series
## Off the Pitch

This chapter looks at plays that complement the pitch, thereby enhancing the effectiveness of the series. The following plays and their effectiveness are analyzed and outlined:

Pitch Pass
Pitch Read
Pitch Trailer
Pitch Screen
Ride
Ride Pass
Ride Charge

### PITCH PASS

#### Play Objective

As the pitch becomes a devastating weapon in an offensive repertoire, defenses begin to cheat on the snap by quick, hard rotation in order to stop it. While quick rotation can't necessarily be considered "cheating," it does tend to create some specific weaknesses in coverage. With the halfback or cornerback coming up hard, the safety must get to the onside third quickly. If he thinks run and begins auxiliary support on the corner, the deep outside third is open. If he gets there quickly, there is an intermediate flat "dead spot" from 10 to 15 yards that cannot be adequately covered. With the offside receiver driving deep, the backside deep third or half must also be covered.

These areas must be exploited by the defense. Once defensive teams know that the Perimeter Attack Offense will throw after the QB has actually made his pitch, they are forced to cover all zones. Forcing the secondary to first respect the pass *after* the pitch leaves the QB's hands makes it easier to run the pitch.

## Coaching Note

Chapter Two discussed the type of athlete needed to man the halfback spot. He does not have to be a top blue-chip athlete with great speed, but it helps if he has enough of an arm to throw the ball deep, and enough accuracy to get the ball in the general area of the 15-yard dead spot.

## Position Responsibilities

*Line*

ONSIDE TACKLE: Pulls as he does in the pitch, attacking the first man to show on the corner, except he attacks the inside breast and does not cross the LOS.

ONSIDE GUARD: Initial movement again is similar to that in the pitch. He takes a lateral step to the onside, checking for any penetration to the frontside gap from a down man, LB, or blitzing secondary man. He must be prepared for penetration from any direction.

If no immediate pressure shows, he wheels the outside foot back so that the hip opens parallel to the backside sideline. He continues to gain depth at a perpendicular to the LOS picking up any backside pressure.

CENTER: Same as onside guard.

OFFSIDE GUARD: Same as onside guard.

OFFSIDE TACKLE: Same as onside guard.

## Receivers

QUICK END:

*If onside:* Similar to the pitch. Blocks the first man to the inside on the line of scrimmage. He must still be conscious of all crackback rules.

*If offside:* Attacks the outside third. If two deep is read, he runs a post; if three deep is read, he splits the middle and outside thirds.

SLOT BACK:

*If onside:* Aggressively fakes normal pitch block inside, but does not make contact with the defender. He then releases to the outside third, reading the coverage. If it looks as if he can beat the man covering the outside third, he continues deep; if not, he breaks an out at a depth of about 15 yards in the dead spot.

*If offside:* Releases on a crossing pattern, working to a depth of about 12 to 15 yards to the farside hook area.

*If in motion to onside:* Goes into motion on the QB's nod. The ball will be snapped as the SB gets to the onside T's position; he attacks the outside third as he does when not in motion and the play is coming to his side.

*If in motion to offside:* The same motion and snap routine will be executed as if to offside, but he sets up for screen.

STRONG END:

*If onside:* If there is motion by the SB to his side, the strong end's job is the same as the quick end's when the QE is onside. If there is no motion, the strong end's job is the same as the SB's when the SB is onside.

*If offside:* Same as the QE when the QE is offside.

## Backfield

QUARTERBACK: Makes the pitch as usual, but then turns back to see if he can help out with any interior or backside penetration.

**Note**

There may be a time, especially if the QB is a good runner, where the QB can be used as a receiver. If this is the case, he releases on a bend to the flat working to a depth of 10 yards, but looks for the ball as soon as he clears the line of scrimmage. In this case, the *onside primary receiver* runs a deep route regardless of secondary coverage. See Diagram 3-1.

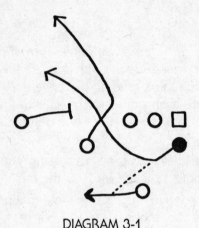

DIAGRAM 3-1

QUICK BACK:

*If onside:* Opens release parallel to the line of scrimmage at top speed, as in the pitch. Once the pitch is made, he continues to fake the run at the perimeter, but immediately tries to pick up the primary receiver. He should be able to read the *bend* route or the deep *jet.* He pulls up and throws. If the routes seem covered, he continues to run. The option priority here is to pass first, run second.

*If offside:* Open steps and follows the QkB; does not fake counter. Once he reaches the onside T-SB seam, he attacks the first man to show. If no one shows, he wheels backside to help out with penetration.

STRONG BACK: Exactly the same as the quick back.

## The Blocking Pattern

### Line

ONSIDE TACKLE: Pulls to inside breast of containment.

ONSIDE GUARD: Onside area pass.

CENTER: Onside area pass.

OFFSIDE GUARD: Onside area pass.

OFFSIDE TACKLE: Onside area pass.

### Receivers

QUICK END:

> *If onside:* Inside on the LOS.
>
> *If offside:* Jet.

SLOT BACK:

> *If onside:* Fake inside, flag or bend.
>
> *If offside:* Cross to far hook.
>
> *If in motion offside:* Screen.
>
> *If in motion onside:* Fake inside, flag or bend.

STRONG END:

> *If onside:* Inside on the LOS if SB is in motion. Fake inside, flag, or bend if SB is not in motion.
>
> *If offside:* Jet.

### Backfield

QUARTERBACK: Pitch, check penetration.

QUICK BACK·

> *If onside:* Fake pitch run and hit jet or bend.
>
> *If offside:* Trail onside back, check penetration.

STRONG BACK: Same as quick back.

## Coaching Note on Change of Primary Receiver

There is a big difference in what is to be expected when the QB is throwing the ball as opposed to the HB. While the QB is given specific reads and is expected to check off to a secondary receiver, the HB has enough problems just pulling up to throw the ball. When his primary receiver is covered, he is to run immediately.

However, when another open receiver is realized, the receiver and route are simply added to the play, and the receiver running that route becomes primary. If it is covered, the HB is to run.

For example:

Pitch Pass, QB Dump
Pitch Pass, TE Jet
Pitch Pass, QE Jet
Pitch Pass, SB Cross

### Base Play Variations and Looks

Diagram 3-2 is the normal pitch pass to the SB (222 pass). The primary pattern for the slot is the *get* or *out,* depending on the read that the slot makes of his coverage. Note the *wheel* technique of the offside tackle. This assumes that there has been no frontside gap penetration. The tackle wheels with his backside foot as he gets his shoulders and hips parallel to the backside sideline.

Diagram 3-3 shows the same pitch pass run to the strong end from the slot with a strong backfield set (221 pass). The line blocking, of course, would not change. The SB crosses to a depth of from 12 to 15 yards through the onside hook area.

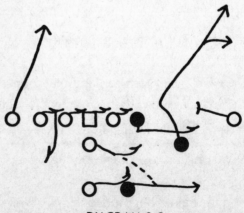

DIAGRAM 3-2

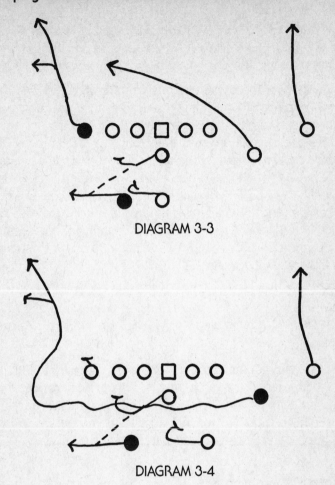

DIAGRAM 3-3

DIAGRAM 3-4

Diagram 3-4 is run from a slot with split backs and mo (221 pass mo). This time it is run to the same side in which the SB is in motion. The strong end should take a split of about 6 yards. The SB fakes inside at first to simulate a run, and then runs the route as described.

**Note**

Later in this chapter, more detail will be given to the line's responsibility and to the blocking pattern. For now, emphasis is being made on the actual patterns and the general play looks.

## PITCH READ

### Play Objective

For many of the same reasons why the *pitch pass* is run, so too is the *pitch read,* except now the QB's ability to throw a quick pass off normal pitch action is taken advantage of.

If the pitch is being run properly, most of the time very quick secondary corner support must take place to stop it. The support most often begins as the QB begins his shuffle step. The pitch read dominantly attacks the 8-yard area of quick passes over the normal QE-SB alignment. If the defender begins up quickly in order to stop the pitch, then he will have difficulty reacting to the pass. If he doesn't come up quickly, he would be able to cover the pass, but have difficulty on the pitch.

### Position Responsibilities

#### Line

ONSIDE TACKLE: Initial movement is similar to that of the other linemen in the pitch pass. He takes a lateral step onside checking for any penetration to the frontside gap from a down man, LB, or blitzing defensive back. He must be prepared for penetration from any direction.

ONSIDE GUARD: Same as onside T.

CENTER: Same as onside T. If there is no immediate pressure, he wheels to the backside on a perpendicular to the LOS.

OFFSIDE GUARD: Same as onside T and center.

OFFSIDE TACKLE: Same as onside T and center.

#### Receivers

QUICK END:

*If onside:* Releases hard favoring the outside as if threatening to drive deep to the third. Reads the defensive halfback or cornerback. If the defensive man drops deep or comes up in, the quick end runs support on his inside shoulder, plants with the inside foot, and runs a 90-degree out at 8 yards. He should expect the ball to be thrown on the break.

If the defender supports the run on his outside shoulder, the QE plants with the outside foot at 9 yards and gives a quick *hook-in,* again expecting the ball to be thrown immediately on the break. If there is a defender in the ball flight line, he slides to the open area to his inside or outside.

*If offside:* Attacks the outside third, but reads two deep or three deep coverage to determine whether to post or seam.

SLOT BACK:

*If onside:* Blocks the outside breast of the first man to show on the line of scrimmage outside the onside tackle's block.

*If offside:* Crosses to the onside hook area to a depth of about 12 to 15 yards.

*If in motion to onside:* Goes into motion on the QB's nod; the ball will be snapped as the SB gets to the onside T's position. He blocks the outside breast of the first man to show on the LOS outside the T's block.

*If in motion to offside:* Sets up for screen.

STRONG END: Exactly the same as the quick end.

## Backfield

QUARTERBACK: Shuffles in normal pitch direction and allows arms to begin pitch fundamental movement, but makes eye contact on DHB immediately on the snap. He makes the same read that the onside end has to make so as to predetermine the type of break on the cut that the end is going to make. He must be cocked and ready to throw just *before* the receiver comes under control at 8 or 9, and release the ball *as* he comes under control. The quick nature of the pass and the release is imperative to the success of the play. If there is a breakdown, he looks to the secondary receivers or runs to daylight.

QUICK BACK:

*If onside:* Attacks the outside breast of the first man to show outside the SB's block.

*If offside:* He should open step, crossover, and plant—he pivots backside to pick up any penetration.

STRONG BACK: Exactly the same as the quick back, except when he blocks to the onside, he will pick up the first man to show outside of the strong tackle's block.

## The Blocking Pattern

### Line

ONSIDE TACKLE: Onside area pass.

ONSIDE GUARD: Onside area pass.

CENTER: Onside area pass.

OFFSIDE GUARD: Onside area pass.

OFFSIDE TACKLE: Onside area pass.

### Receivers

QUICK END:

> *If onside:* Reads corner for hook or out at 8.
>
> *If offside:* Jet.

SLOT BACK:

> *If onside:* First man outside T's block.
>
> *If offside:* Crosses to far hook area.
>
> *If in motion onside:* First man outside T's block.
>
> *If in motion offside:* Screen.

STRONG END: Same as quick end.

### Backfield

QUARTERBACK: Fakes pitch, reads corner for hook or out.

QUICK BACK:

> *If onside:* First man outside SB.
>
> *If offside:* Trail and play backside penetration.

STRONG BACK: Same as quick back.

## Coaching Notes on Play Variations

### Pitch slot read

This play is run exactly like the pitch read, except now the SB takes the job of the QE, and the QE blocks the first man to show to his inside on the LOS. Everything else in the play remains the same. This play, of course, would not be run with motion. This can prove most effective when the defensive corner keys the QE, who is blocking down.

Generally, when the typical block the QE makes in the pitch is one where he attacks the outside third, then the *pitch read* is most effective. However, when his normal block is to block down, then the *pitch slot read* would be better.

### Pitch trailer

This is the old "hook and trailer" play, which comes nicely off the pitch read action. The QE, however, always *hooks in.* If someone is in the ball flight line, then he slides to the open area as normal and the "trailer" is off. If the ball is thrown on the hook and fielded cleanly in the hands of the end, he makes the trail-pitch to the onside back. Otherwise, he turns upfield as on a normal pass reception.

The end makes the trail-pitch with "butt stuck back into the secondary," keeping a wide base and a low center of gravity. In this manner, even if he gets hit from behind when making the pitch, it should have no effect on the movement of the ball, since the defender would have difficulty immediately controlling the end's arms. Complete responsibility here for not fumbling is in the hands of the end.

The onside HB, instead of blocking on the LOS, attacks right outside the last man on the LOS on a direct angle about 3 yards outside the hook of the end. He should *never* slow up, but be prepared to take the lateral at top speed.

The QB should have time to throw the ball to the quick side because of the block of the SB on the LOS. To the strong side, it may prove beneficial to operate from a strong backfield alignment.

## Base Play Variations and Looks

### Note

As already mentioned in the pitch pass, the specific blocking schemes versus various fronts will be handled a little later.

Diagram 3-5 shows slot left, split backs, pitch read left, or 121 read. Note the emphasis on protection for the QB. This prevents the possibility of a QB sack if the QE is covered and also simulates pitch action in the corner. This effect would generally force the primary containment defender not to come up until *after* the actual pitch is made. However, experience has shown us that any hesitation by that defender makes it most difficult to stop the pitch. Here we are assuming that the offside guard has no penetration and wheels backside. The QE's break, whether out or hook, depends on his read of the corner support. The QB shuffles as he does in the pitch, but levels off, all the while keying support as does the QE. As he levels off, his arm is cocked to throw.

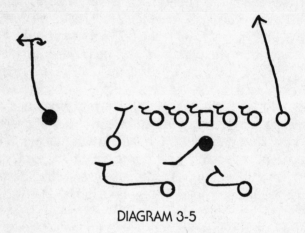

DIAGRAM 3-5

However, if in a particular game, the QE generally blocks down on the pitch, as is often the case, the pitch slot read would be more effective. Diagram 3-6 illustrates 121 slot read.

Diagram 3-7 shows the pitch trailer when run to the quick side, and Diagram 3-8 shows the same play run to the strong side. When run to the strong side, the strong end will *hook out* if aligned tight, and will *hook in* if aligned wide. Note how the strong back will really take the SB's place as a blocker when the play is run to the strong side. For this reason, a weak backfield set is important when the play is run strong. Diagram 3-7 is 121 trailer, while Diagram 3-8 is 122 trailer.

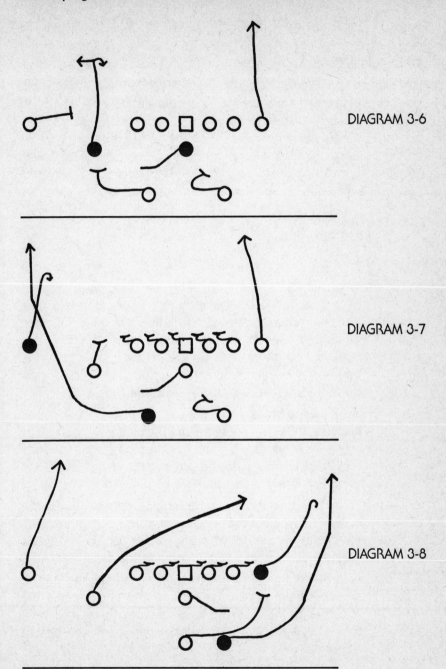

DIAGRAM 3-6

DIAGRAM 3-7

DIAGRAM 3-8

## PITCH SCREEN

### Play Objective

The *pitch screen* will always be set up opposite pitch, pitch pass, and pitch read action. With the emphasis that defenses must place on defending these actions to one side, this offside screen can often be a game breaker if not respected by the defense. Forcing teams to play the screen and to be conscious of it also prevents them from overplaying the actual pitch side, and once again, enhances the base effectiveness of the attack.

### Position Responsibilities

#### *Line*

ONSIDE TACKLE: Sets up in normal onside area pass technique to the pitch side, but once the hitting position is set, he does not move his feet. He continues a bonafide effort to block the defender, but as long as his feet don't move, the block won't be held. As the defender slides past, he releases to the screen area, taking the first man to show on the corner, and attacks his outside breast.

If there is no pressure, he gives a 101, 101-101, 102 count, then releases. If there is pressure, but the defensive man never slides past, he works for screenside leverage position on the man, but doesn't release to the screen area, thereby allowing the defender to easily read screen.

ONSIDE GUARD: Exactly the same technique and rule as the onside tackle, but on the release to the screen area, he checks to the inside for a LB, DE, or safety, who reads screen and tries to force it from the inside.

CENTER: Exactly the same technique and rule as the onside tackle, except on the release to the screen area, he checks into the offensive backfield area, being prepared to pick up any "garbage" that may have read screen from the offensive side of the line of scrimmage.

OFFSIDE GUARD: Blocks his normal onside area pass technique to the pitch side. Blocks as usual, but does not allow penetration.

OFFSIDE TACKLE: Same as onside guard.

## Receivers

QUICK END:

*If onside:* Takes a hard three-step release beginning with and ending with the outside foot, plants and comes back across the LOS. He plays the ball and attacks the outside breast of the first man to show in containment, unless the onside tackle is not yet in position to attack the perimeter; in this case, except to cut inside his block as he gets to the corner. Whenever the T is late getting to the corner, he will wind up kicking his man out.

*If offside:* Runs the hook at a depth of about 8 yards.

SLOT BACK:

*If onside:* If screen is going to the QE, releases deep on a jet.

*If offside:* If screen is going to the strong end, blocks as normal on a pitch read.

*If in motion to offside:* Blocks the outside breast of the first man to show on the LOS outside the T's block. Remember that the screen is being run to the QE.

## Coaching Note

This play generally would not be run to the strong side with SB motion to the screen, basically because timing between the route of the SB and the strong end would not be good. While it could be coached, it probably would not be worth the time proportionate to its actual use.

STRONG END: Same as for the quick end.

## Backfield

QUARTERBACK: Executes pitch read action away from the screen; he must be sure to have respectable depth by shuffling out and setting deeper than usual. It is then the QB's responsibility to get the ball to the receiver. If the QB feels he has to put too much of an arc on the ball, the throw shouldn't be made. Keep in mind that this is more of an upward-crossfield screen, as opposed to a typical screen off straight dropback action; consequently, the danger of someone picking the ball off if the screen is read too early is greater.

If there's a question of getting the ball to the receiver, the QB should run. He does not check off to another receiver, since a lineman may already be downfield.

QUICK BACK:

*If onside:* Attacks the inside breast of the first man to show outside the SB's block.

*If offside:* Comes across as in the pitch read, but sets up closer to the LOS and more to the pitch side than normal, thereby not becoming an impediment to the screen itself.

STRONG BACK: Same as the quick back.

## The Blocking Pattern

*Line*

ONSIDE TACKLE: Screen release to containment.

ONSIDE GUARD: Screen release to force.

CENTER: Screen release to "garbage."

OFFSIDE GUARD: Onside area pass.

OFFSIDE TACKLE: Onside area pass.

*Receivers*

QUICK END:

*If onside:* Release, come back for screen.

*If offside:* Hook at 8.

SLOT BACK:

*If onside:* Jet.

*If offside:* First man outside T's block.

*If in motion offside:* First man outside T's block.

STRONG END: Same as quick end.

*Backfield*

QUARTERBACK: Set up for pitch read, execute screen.

QUICK BACK:

> *If onside:* First man outside the SB's block.
>
> *If offside:* Trail and play frontside penetration.

STRONG BACK: Same as quick back.

## Coaching Note on Play Variation

*Pitch slot screen*

This play is run exactly like the pitch screen except the SB and the QE switch responsibilities.

## Base Play Variations and Looks

Diagram 3-9 is a 222 screen. Remember that the StE ideally wants to attack outside of containment in the outside hip of the T. However, if the T gets there late, he will kick containment out, and the StE will break inside of that kickout block, and then get back to the outside, so as to avoid the pursuit. Note also that the QB drops deeper after his shuffle than he does in the pitch read. Should the T feel that he must stay with his original defender at the LOS, the G will attack containment.

In Diagram 3-10, 221 slot screen is run. Here the QE and the SB simply switch responsibilities.

Diagram 3-11 shows the pitch screen being run to the QE with motion. The play is 221 screen mo.

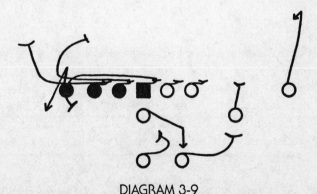

DIAGRAM 3-9

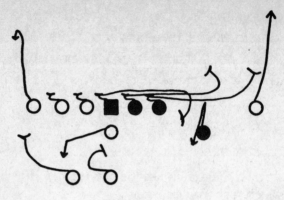

DIAGRAM 3-10

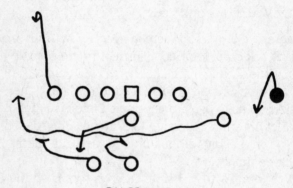

DIAGRAM 3-11

## RIDE

### Play Objective

When defenses have been effective stopping the pitch, they have done so with quick containment on the corner and good aggressive pursuit from the inside. The ride forces someone to play the responsibility of the off-tackle seam, at least initially.

If the defensive pursuit is too quick, generally either the off-tackle or the dive hole will be open. This is the area the ride takes advantage of

## Position Responsibilities

### Line

ONSIDE TACKLE: Aggressively blocks the first man to show beginning head up, then works his way outside. If no one shows as a threat to the play between himself and the SB (or strong end), then he attacks the first man to his inside.

ONSIDE GUARD: Blocks as he would in the pitch—onside area run.

CENTER: Same as the onside guard.

OFFSIDE GUARD: Same as the onside guard.

OFFSIDE TACKLE: Works hard to get to the track.

### Receivers

QUICK END:

*If onside:* Releases to the track.

*If offside:* Releases to the track.

SLOT BACK:

*If onside:* Aggressively attacks the first man to show from a head-up position to an inside seam. If no one shows, he releases to the nearest LB.

*If offside:* Track.

*If in motion to onside:* Attacks the first man to show outside the T's block; the ball should be snapped by the time the SB gets to the G-T seam.

*If in motion to offside:* Fake screen.

STRONG END: Same as SB.

### Backfield

QUARTERBACK: Opens shuffle as in normal pitch action, but he must be sure to get more depth. It is the shuffle itself that should come out on a deeper angle, bringing the QB to a mesh point with the offside back somewhere in the G-T seam. He plants and makes the handoff, then fakes an attack on the perimeter.

*Backfield*

QUARTERBACK: Fakes pitch, rides handoff, attacks perimeter.

FAKE BACK: Pitch.

RIDE BACK: Reads daylight on outside T path.

## Base Play Variations and Looks

Diagrams 3-12 and 3-13 show the ride being run to the quick and strong sides, respectively. In both cases, a backfield set should be used where the running back operates from a normal fullback set. This is important for timing. If he is in a split backfield set, *fly* or setback motion should be used. Note in both plays that the QB is to plant while he makes a long, riding handoff. He then attacks the corner. This will set up the ride pass. Diagram 3-12 is 123 and Diagram 3-13 is 124.

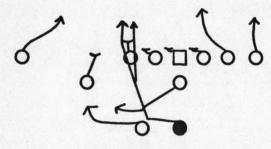

DIAGRAM 3-12

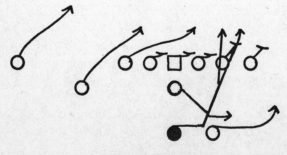

DIAGRAM 3-13

QUICK BACK:

*If fake back:* Fakes pitch action.

*If ride back:* From the FB position, he should open, crossover, and plant, exploding hard to the outside hip of the onside tackle. Once in the proper path of that outside hip, he must check the inside hip for daylight. If it's there, he breaks to that inside hip hard. Otherwise, he bangs ahead with everything he has.

STRONG BACK: Same as quick back.

## The Blocking Pattern

*Line*

ONSIDE TACKLE: On, outside, inside, LB.

ONSIDE GUARD: Onside area run.

CENTER: Onside area run.

OFFSIDE GUARD: Onside area run.

OFFSIDE TACKLE: Track.

*Receivers*

QUICK END:

*If onside:* Track.

*If offside:* Track.

SLOT BACK:

*If onside:* On, inside.

*If offside:* Track.

*If in motion onside:* First man outside T's block.

*If in motion offside:* Screen.

STRONG END: Same as for SB.

## RIDE PASS

## Play Objective

This play, when taken in light of the rest of the series, is probably the most difficult to stop. Deep, intermediate, and short zones must be covered, and the perimeter must be contained. This is a run-pass or pass-run option on the perimeter. Whether the run or pass is considered as the priority here depends on the type of QB the offense has.

A healthy ride fake will hold the defenders inside, and there is never hesitation on the QB's part as he moves to the sideline.

## Position Responsibilities

### Line

ONSIDE TACKLE: Blocks anyone head up and then goes to a normal onside area pass rule, except he must be completely aggressive (without going downfield) in order to simulate run; he does not wheel.

ONSIDE GUARD: Onside area pass without a wheel.

CENTER: Normal onside area pass.

OFFSIDE GUARD: Same as center.

OFFSIDE TACKLE: Same as center.

### Receivers

QUICK END:

*If onside:* Flag.

*If offside:* Jet.

SLOT BACK:

*If onside:* Blocks on, and then onside area pass. SB serves as a blocker.

*If offside:* Drags to a depth of 12 to 15 yards in for hook.

*If in motion to onside:* Runs a swing route outside the end's normal alignment.

*If in motion to offside:* Sets up for a screen.

STRONG END: Same as quick end.

### Backfield

QUARTERBACK: Begins pitch shuffle and then fakes ride handoff. Execution here is critical; it must not be a poor fake.

The QB should extend his arms as deep as possible to meet the back and ride that fake to his front hip.

After the fake, he gains one step for depth and begins the attack on the perimeter. The first key should be the TD deep. If the end is open, he pulls up and throws. If the end is covered, he continues a top-speed attack to the corner and dumps off to the swing back, who has already turned upfield, if the defense contains the quarterback.

If the swing back is covered, the ride back is probably open on a *go* route through the onside hook area. However, if the fake was a good one, the ride back should be tackled.

The QB does not hesitate; if in doubt, he runs.

QUICK BACK:

*If swing back:* Fakes pitch action, then releases well outside the normal end's position and "swings" up the field. If he reads the QB on a definite run, he attacks the outside breast of the first man to show on the corner.

*If ride back:* Fakes ride as if he has the ball; he should expect to get hit on the LOS. This time he attacks only the outside hip of the tackle—he stays outside and does not bend inside to daylight.

If he is still on his feet, he does a go route through the normal onside hook area looking for the ball over his outside shoulder. If QB commits to run, he attacks the first man to show.

STRONG BACK: Same as the quick back, except if the SB is in motion to his side (which is the onside), then he attacks the first man to show the T's block.

## The Blocking Pattern

*Line*

ONSIDE TACKLE: On, aggressive onside area pass.

ONSIDE GUARD: Aggressive onside area pass.

CENTER: Onside area pass.

OFFSIDE GUARD: Onside area pass.

OFFSIDE TACKLE: Onside area pass.

*Receivers*

QUICK END:

> *If onside:* Flag.
>
> *If offside:* Jet.

SLOT BACK:

> *If onside:* On, aggressive onside area pass.
>
> *If offside:* Drag to far hook.
>
> *If in motion onside:* Swing.
>
> *If in motion offside:* Screen.

STRONG END: Same as quick end.

*Backfield*

QUARTERBACK: Fakes ride and attacks perimeter, thinking *deep, run,* and *dump.*

SWING BACK: Pitch, swing.

RIDE BACK: Ride, go.

## Coaching Notes on Play Variations

### *Ride pass Sam*

This is executed the exact same way as the normal ride pass, except the HB blocks the first man to show outside the T's block, and the SB "bends" an out to about 10 yards, after an initial inside release. This will not be run with motion.

### *Ride pass jet—Ride pass go*

Again, these are both run exactly like the ride pass, except the QB is being alerted to different primary receivers. Here the QB primarily thinks *pass.* On the *ride pass jet,* the offside end is primary. On the *ride pass go,* the faking ride back is primary. The QB fakes the ride as usual, but pulls up to pass. When these plays are called, it is because those routes are expected to be open.

### Ride pass charge

Action looks like ride pass, but there is no pass option. It is most effective because the defense is still forced to defend a pass threat.

LINE BLOCKING PATTERN: Onside area run.

SB BLOCKING PATTERN:

> *If onside:* First man outside T's block.
>
> *If offside:* Track.
>
> *If in motion onside:* First man outside T's block.
>
> *If in motion offside:* Screen.

END'S BLOCKING PATTERN:

> *If onside:* Flag.
>
> *If offside:* Track.

SWING BACK'S BLOCKING PATTERN: Attacks outside breast of first man to show outside T's or SB's block.

QUARTERBACK'S BLOCKING PATTERN: Fakes ride; attacks the outside breast of the first man to show on the corner.

### Ride pass slot

This is exactly the same as the ride pass, except the SB and the QE switch responsibilities. The SB flags, while the QE blocks the first to show on the corner.

## Base Play Variations and Looks

Diagram 3-14 is 123 pass. Remember that the QB's first read is deep for the score. If he has that, he pulls up and throws. If not, he attacks the corner using the swing back as a safety valve dump. If he does dump the ball off, he does so on the run. If "jet" or "go" is called, the QB pulls up after he begins his corner attack to make those throws. If the StB is not tackled, he continues his go route. However, expect him to be tackled.

Diagram 3-15 shows 123 pass Sam, where the QkB blocks for the SB, and the SB bends an out route after an inside release.

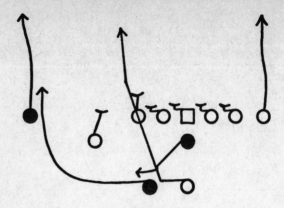

DIAGRAM 3-14

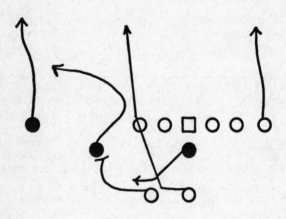

DIAGRAM 3-15

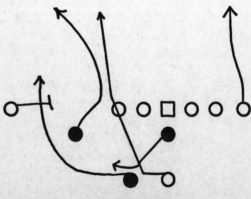

DIAGRAM 3-16

Diagram 3-16 illustrates 123 pass slot, where the QE and the SB switch responsibilities. This has proven very effective since the QE's action simulates a run read for the perimeter containment. Whether ride pass or ride pass slot is used in a game really depends on the type of blocking you are making on the corner that week.

Note that in all cases for the ride pass and variations, the StB stays on a path on the outside hip of the T. He does not veer inside as he may in the ride.

## THE PITCH AND RIDE SERIES
## VERSUS SEVEN-MAN DEFENSIVE FRONTS

Diagram 3-17 shows the pitch pass against a base fifty look. Keep in mind that a penetrating technique by the DT in an effort to knock down the pitch has proven most ineffective. Against the onside area run blocking schemes, if the DT pinches inside he will be picked up by the onside G. The movement of the DT has generally been on a line either on the LOS or on a pursuit angle away from it. He generally takes himself out of the play. If the nose slants frontside, he will be picked up by the C; if he slants offside, the offside G will take him. The offside T will step frontside for any penetration there. If he gets none, he will pivot back to pick up the offside DT. If the offside G gets no pressure, he will wheel backside.

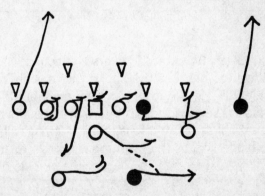

DIAGRAM 3-17

## Coaching Note

It is also very important to keep in mind that one third of the time the ball is snapped on "set," thereby taking advantage of the two-point stance for the lateral movement of the line. In practice, however, these techniques are generally drilled from a down stance.

In Diagram 3-18, the pitch slot read is run to the right versus an offset fifty stack. The only real difference here from the pitch pass is that the onside T doesn't pull; instead, he reaches on the onside DT, while the C does the same with the nose. If the onside G doesn't get any frontside penetration, he will privot back inside and help double the nose. The offside G reaches frontside to play any possible penetration from a stunt, and then pivots back to help out on the backside DT. If the G sees the offside T has the DT by himself, he wheels. If there is doubt, he stays with him on a double-team.

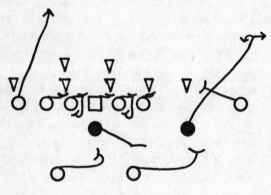

DIAGRAM 3-18

Diagram 3-19 shows the ride versus a college 4-3 look. The only real difference here for the line is that onside T blocks on, outside, inside, LB. He does *not* block an area, but the man who first enters into the sequence of his blocking pattern. In this case, he will block the LB. If the LB tightens to the LOS, he will become on or outside, depending on his alignment relative to the QT. The running back stays on a path in line with the outside hip of the T's alignment, *unless* he reads daylight inside; then he breaks there. Here the rest of the line blocks zone frontside in a run technique; namely, the onside area run, except for the offside T, who tries to get to the track, but never allows a defender to cross his face. In this case, had the backside LB already crossed the offside T's face, he would continue directly to the track.

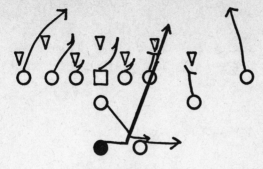

DIAGRAM 3-19

Blocking for the ride pass is exactly the same in principle as the pitch read, except the onside T blocks his man aggressively as determined by his blocking pattern. The fake of the ride back makes his block easier. The initial steps for the line on pitch screen are also identical to the pitch read.

## THE PITCH AND RIDE SERIES
## VERSUS EIGHT-MAN DEFENSIVE FRONTS

All these plays are run to the left.

Diagram 3-20 shows the pitch read versus a split-4; Diagram 3-21 illustrates the ride against a gap-4; and Diagram 3-22 is the ride pass versus a gap-8.

Versus the split-4, the frontside G and T pick up the frontside DT and DE, while the strong back takes the outside LB. If there is a

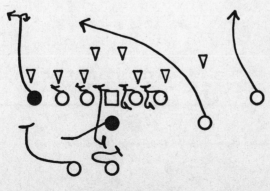

DIAGRAM 3-20

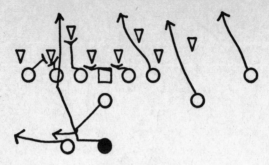

DIAGRAM 3-21

stunt from the middle LBs, the C and the offside guard will handle it. If there is not, the C wheels, and the offside G pivots to pick up the DT. If the offside T sees the G has the DT, he pivots to play the DE.

In the ride against the gap-4, the onside T blocks on, outside, and finds the DT. The StE blocks on, inside, and doubles the DT. The rest of the line blocks the onside area run with the offside T getting to the track. Assuming the StB reads daylight inside, his cut is to the inside hip of the T, as he breaks upfield on a perpendicular to the LOS. The problem here is if the C can't get to the frontside DT. Should this be the case, the C will employ his *seal rule,* which will be explained at the end of the chapter.

In Diagram 3-22, 123 pass versus a gap-8, the entire line blocks the onside area pass, except for the aggressive man block by the onside T. There should be no wheels here since there is frontside pressure at every seam. Since the QB attacks the corner,

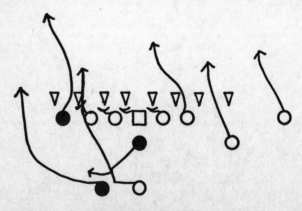

DIAGRAM 3-22

backside pressure should not be a problem. Since the ride back is given a long ball fake and veers off-tackle, the frontside DE should bite. If he does not, the pitch back will attack the DE's outside breast after first faking the pitch. The strong end then reads his coverage and either attacks deep or breaks off an out at 12. To do this, a *load* call is made in the huddle or at the LOS by the QB. Without it, the QB should still have time to get the ball off.

## COACHING NOTES ON THESE BLOCKING SCHEMES

### Note One

Keep in mind that in both of these series, the objective is to attack the defensive perimeter (or off-T as in the case on the ride). All initial backfield action comes directly off the pitch. As discussed in Chapter Two, blitzing LB's and inside penetration stunts have *never* hurt the pitch and have proven ineffective in stopping it. Consequently, we have seen very little of this type of defensive action over the years. The first prerequisite of the rest of the series is to avoid penetration. The onside area run and pass concepts are most effective in this regard.

### Note Two

As long as I have been around football, just reading about blocking schemes doesn't always make 100 percent sense. Most of the time, answering questions is necessary for real understanding. As the reader, be patient if things don't at first seem crystal clear. The blocking patterns discussed here and throughout the book *have been proven* most effective. It takes a thorough understanding of the offense to see this. Hang in there, Coach, it will be worth your time!

## THE SEAL RULE

On any onside area run or pass rule, there comes a time, as in the case of the C in Diagram 3-21, where he can prevent penetration by the DT, but not prevent the DT's pursuit to the POA. When this happens, the offensive player simply tells his teammate *"seal,"* in which case the neighbor blocks down and seals the defender. The player, who originally had the problem, reaches around the neighbor's block. See Diagram 3-23 for the ride blocking against the gap-4 with a "seal" call by the C.

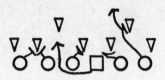

DIAGRAM 3-23

Note that when this is called the neighbor of the player with the "problem" never has an immediate defender head up or in his frontside gap on the LOS. If he does, the player with the "problem defender" will be able to run his opponent right down the LOS into a pileup and still prevent defensive penetration. It is, as in the case in Diagram 3-21, when there is a problem.

Most of the time when there is a problem, it is the center who has it. This is because he must (1) always begin down, and (2) always snap the ball. Consequently, he doesn't have the mobility of the linemen.

# 4

# Attacking the
# Quick Pursuit Defenses

In the years that we have run the pitch, the only way defenses have stopped it has been with hard, aggressive containment on the corner and good, quick pursuit from the inside. The onside area run blocking rule and coordinated technique have proven penetrating and blitzing defensive interiors to be ineffective. The lack of pursuit that the penetrating front gives allows an attractive running lane on the corner, even when containment takes place quickly.

This chapter explains how the perimeter attack takes advantage of the quick pursuit defenses with a reverse, counter, and misdirection game. The following plays are analyzed and outlined:

> Reverse
> Reverse Pass
> Pitch Trap
> Pitch Trap Boat

## REVERSE

### Play Objective

The theory here is to have a quick hitting, explosive misdirection play that comes precisely off the pitch. As teams pursue and rotate to the pitch, the backsides become vulnerable. Because of the nature of the play, this is run to the strong side only.

## Position Responsibilities

### Line

QUICK TACKLE: Plays normal onside area run.

QUICK GUARD: Same as onside tackle.

CENTER: Same as onside tackle.

STRONG GUARD: Takes a deep drop-step in behind the center. He must remember that the center is blocking to the onside, which is in the opposite direction of the strong guard's step. The SG allows his weight and body lean to shift to that inside foot. This simulates a pull in the direction of the pitch and provides a false key to the offside LB. This will also put the guard in a better blocking relationship with the running back.

He pushes off that inside foot and open steps to the onside. He attacks the inside breast of the first defender to show outside the strong end's block.

STRONG TACKLE: Aggressively attacks the first man to the inside on the line of scrimmage. He does not go inside the normal alignment of the strong guard. The center, blocking the proper onside area run technique, and the initial influence movement of the strong guard will handle any defender on the line of scrimmage in this area.

If there is no one on the line of scrimmage in this area, he attacks the LB.

### Receivers

STRONG END: Assignment is very similar to that of the strong tackle's. He blocks the first man to the inside on the line of scrimmage. He does not go inside the normal alignment of the strong tackle. If no one is there, he attacks the LB.

QUICK END: Fakes block to the inside. This simulates the pitch. He begins with the inside foot. On the third step, he attacks the backside third or half. He checks out the way he is covered by the defensive secondary off this action.

SLOT BACK: Alignment cannot be wider than 3 yards from the tackle. If alignment is wider, motion will be necessary. He takes a deep lateral release inside. Depth must be gained on the initial steps. He receives the handoff from the QB, and think daylight just outside the strong end's block. He should try to hit the line of scrimmage on a particular.

As long as assignments are executed properly, he should be one-on-one with that side defensive half or corner.

### Backfield

QUARTERBACK: He opens and shuffles as in the pitch, except he stays closer to the line of scrimmage. On the shuffle, he pivots the lead foot and swings the back foot around. His back should now be parallel to the scrimmage line.

He makes the handoff while he is in this position. After the handoff, he explodes to the corner, gaining depth. He checks the pass defensive coverage to that side.

QUICK BACK: Fakes pitch, but continues on course and runs a swing upfield. He should check how the defense plays him.

STRONG BACK: Trails the pitch fake by the quick back. He must be sure not to interfere with the slot back. As he passes the QB-SB exchange point, he attacks the outside breast of the first man to show on the corner. He must note who is responsible for containment here, since this will be his job on the reverse pass.

## The Blocking Pattern

### Line

QUICK TACKLE: Onside area run.

QUICK GUARD: Onside area run.

CENTER: Onside area run.

STRONG GUARD: False key. Attacks the first defender to show outside the strong end's block.

STRONG TACKLE: First man inside on the LOS, but not inside the strong guard. If no one, LB.

## Receivers

STRONG END: First man inside on the LOS, but not inside the strong tackle. If no one, LB.

QUICK END: Fakes pitch. Attacks outside third. Checks coverage.

SLOT BACK: Releases inside. Takes handoff. Finds daylight outside strong end's block.

## Backfield

QUARTERBACK: Fakes pitch. Exchanges with slot back. Attacks corner. Checks coverage.

QUICK BACK: Fakes pitch. Swings. Checks coverage.

STRONG BACK: Trails pitch. Attacks containment.

## Play Look

See Diagram 4-1 for 225 (slot right, reverse left) against a base Oklahoma. With the emphasis placed on the pitch and the attack on the corner, the blocks by the OG and StT on the linebackers are feasible. Experience has shown that the LB to the side of the pitch will start to move outside. While the other LB won't leave as hard, he does at least lean playside, and this "lean" allows the T to make his

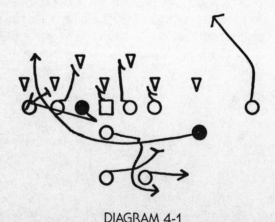

DIAGRAM 4-1

block. It is important to note, however, that the StT must step laterally inside on the LOS, in order to first clear the DT so he can get to the LB.

## REVERSE PASS

### Play Objective

There is no doubt that the reverse has been a very explosive play over the years. However, defenses can stop it as long as they key the slot back reverse action and play a disciplined backside game that holds and expects offensive misdirection.

The *reverse pass* is geared as an attack on the corner off reverse action. When a defense effectively stops the reverse, it is generally because they are well-coached, read it early, and react to it swiftly. The reverse pass exploits this reaction, and once again, puts tremendous pressure on the perimeter.

Since the reverse can be run only to the strong side, the reverse pass will be run only to the quick side.

### Position Responsibilities

#### Line

QUICK TACKLE: Executes normal onside area pass. Note that the onside for the reverse pass is outside. The onside for the reverse is inside.

QUICK GUARD: Same as the quick tackle.

CENTER: Same as the quick tackle.

STRONG GUARD: Executes as on the reverse, but he must be sure not to go downfield on his pull to the outside.

STRONG TACKLE: Executes normal onside area pass. He shouldn't worry about the wheel technique, since the strong guard will be pulling behind him.

#### Receivers

STRONG END: Same as the strong tackle. We do not want the strong end downfield, since we wish to simulate the run. However, if the strong end reads the defensive half or corner so committing to the run that he gets to the line of scrimmage, he may release toward the outside third after executing initial onside area pass steps.

If, after his release, he is wide open, we will predetermine him as the primary receiver the next time we run the reverse pass (reverse pass—strong end check).

QUICK END: Releases to the inside stimulating the pitch, as done in the reverse. Breaks to the outside third reading the coverage on a jet. If he has done a good job of reading the secondary play on the reverse, he should be well-prepared mentally to read and attack this coverage.

SLOT BACK: Takes an inside release as normal on the reverse. He must be sure not to slow up after the fake. He passes the QB with a slight bend in the upfield shoulder to better disguise the ball.

If the fake is executed properly, people will attract to him. The SB must be prepared to attack the first defender to show on his side of the line of scrimmage. He should expect a defender to the offside of the center. If no one is there, he continues on his course. He does *not* slow up.

## Backfield

QUARTERBACK: Executes normal reverse steps. Gives a good, long ride fake to the SB. Pulls the ball as the SB reaches his backside hip. He must remember that his back is parallel to the line of scrimmage.

As the ball is pulled, he gains depth as he aggressively attacks the corner. If "strong end check" was called, he pulls up and reads the strong end to the backside. If he is not open or if he has not released, he looks to the frontside. If the StE is open, the QB gets the ball to him. This will probably not have to be thrown very far due to the strong end's initial play.

If "strong end check" was not called, he should key the quick end on a jet first. If he is open, the QB pulls up and throws. This is probably a touchdown. If he is not open, the QB continues his attack on the corner as a pass-run option. The quick back on a swing is almost always open.

If containment forces the QB to pull up, he still makes the same frontside reads on his two patterns. If contained, and if both patterns are covered, it is easy to get the ball out of bounds because of the swing route of the quick back.

QUICK BACK: As in the reverse, he fakes pitch, then runs the swing. He should know what to expect here in terms of coverage if he has been checking coverage on the reverse.

He keeps his width on the route as he swings upfield, unless he is overplayed from the outside. Then, he takes advantage of the huge seam to his inside by breaking inside.

STRONG BACK: Executes as in the reverse. Does not interfere with QB-SB exchange. Attacks aggressively the outside breast of the first man to show outside the quick tackle's block.

## The Blocking Pattern

### Line

QUICK TACKLE: Onside area pass.

QUICK GUARD: Onside area pass.

CENTER: Onside area pass.

STRONG GUARD: Reverse block. No downfield.

STRONG TACKLE: Onside area pass. No wheel.

### Receivers

STRONG END: Onside area pass. No wheel. Checks secondary corner support.

QUICK END: Fakes reverse. Jet.

SLOT BACK: Fakes reverse. Blocks backside aggressively.

### Backfield

QUARTERBACK: Fakes reverse. Attacks corner. Reads outside third first.

QUICK BACK: Fakes reverse. Swings.

STRONG BACK: Attacks containment

## Base Play Look and Variations

See Diagram 4-2 for the reverse pass from a slot left, 126 pass, against a base forty defense. If the backside DT crashes immediately, he will probably run into the StG, who is pulling to fake the reverse. If the DT manages to avoid the StG and penetrates, he will be blocked by the LB. If the C gets no frontside pressure, he will pivot back to check for that DT also. If the StE reads quick support by the secondary to his side, he will attack the outside third, and later on will run the strong end check.

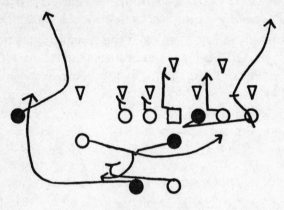

DIAGRAM 4-2

## PITCH TRAP

### Play Objective

Simple containment on the corner will never be enough to stop the pitch. To stop it, quick and aggressive containment on the corner *must* turn the play back inside into the forcing agents or inside pursuit.

A good inside LB often pressures the pitch from the inside. In order to do this he must read quickly and get out there fast. The *pitch trap* then is geared to take advantage of the quick lateral movement that an inside LB must take if he is to react to and force the pitch.

## Position Responsibilities

### Line

ONSIDE TACKLE: Pulls to simulate pitch.

ONSIDE GUARD: Blocks the first man on the line of scrimmage to his inside. He does not go any further than a normal nose guard position. If no one is on the line of scrimmage to the inside, he will influence pull outside. This will generally prevent any reading DT from squeezing down inside. If the DT does not generally read, he blocks head up and then goes outside after checking that no one is inside.

CENTER: Blocks the first man to the backside, regardless of whether or not he is on or off the line. Versus a nose guard, he folds behind the onside guard, who is blocking down, and gets to the frontside LB.

OFFSIDE GUARD: Pulls inside taking the first odd jersey to show. He gains depth on the first step to clear the C. Then he angles up toward the scrimmage line. If the first defender has "overpenetrated," he then turns upfield hard. He *never* hesitates at or near the point of attack. He must also remember that there is no rule prohibiting clipping in this zone on this pull.

OFFSIDE TACKLE: Fills inside hard for the pulling guard. He must not allow any defender to chase the puller or to penetrate the line of scrimmage.

### Receivers

QUICK END:

*If onside or offside:* Blocks as he normally would block the pitch. This will simulate the pitch if inside, and will simulate the pitch trap boot if offside. In either case it may hold the outside perimeter people for an extra count. This would then increase the chances of a breakaway if the runner can clear the LB area.

SLOT BACK:

*If onside or offside:* Blocks the same as the quick end for the same reasons.

*If in motion to onside or offside:* Goes into motion on QB's nod at top speed. On the snap, he turns upfield quickly and attacks the first defender to show. He should expect the runner to cut back in behind him if he clears the LB area.

STRONG END:

*If onside or offside:* Blocks exactly the same as the quick end.

## Backfield

QUARTERBACK: Opens to the midline. He uses both body lean and "ball swing" to simulate pitch. He brings the back foot around in a full swing, and pivots back to face the runner as he runs at the point of attack. While the point of attack is basically the runner's responsibility, the QB must know where it is also. This will affect exactly where he pivots to. After the handoff, he attacks the corner to simulate the pitch trap boot later on.

QUICK BACK:

*If onside:* Fakes the pitch.

*If offside:* The QkB is the runner. On alignment, he determines where the point of attack will actually be. Versus an odd defense, the back will cut upfield off the onside guard's butt. He must remember that the onside guard is blocking down. The same will be true versus a gap defense. Versus more of an even look, he attacks the inside foot of the center's alignment.

He will open step, then begin upfield cut to point of attack. While this cut may begin on an angle, he must work hard at being on a perpendicular to the line of scrimmage by the time he gets to the handoff exchange point. Unless aligned in a normal FB position, this may mean his alignment should be cheated inside and deeper.

STRONG BACK:

*If onside or offside:* Same as the quick back.

## The Blocking Pattern

### Line

ONSIDE TACKLE: Pulls as in pitch.

ONSIDE GUARD: Inside on the line, influences pull outside.

CENTER: First man backside. Folds frontside versus a nose.

OFFSIDE GUARD: Trap.

OFFSIDE TACKLE: Fill.

### Receivers

QUICK END:

*If onside or offside:* Blocks pitch.

SLOT BACK:

*If onside or offside:* Blocks pitch.

*If in motion to onside or offside:* Runs interference downfield.

STRONG END:

*If onside or offside:* Blocks pitch.

### Backfield

QUARTERBACK: Fakes pitch; pivots back for handoff; attacks the corner.

QUICK BACK:

*If onside:* Fakes pitch.

*If offside:* Finds point of attack. Open steps, plants, and attacks upfield.

STRONG BACK:

*If onside or offside:* Same as quick back.

## Base Play Variations and Looks

Diagrams 4-3, 4-4, and 4-5 show the pitch trap from a slot right (228) against gap, even, and odd defensive schemes.

Keep in mind that in Diagram 4-3, the pulling G will attack the DE (aligned just outside of the QT), should the DE react inside. However, the G is coached to pull on an angle across the LOS. We assume the DE will react to the pitch. The runner will probably break inside the frontside LB, since he is also expected to react to the pitch. If he has cleared out of there, the G will look back inside to the offside LB, who is really the problem.

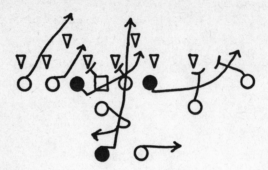

DIAGRAM 4-3

In Diagram 4-4, it is again assumed that the inside DT, DE, and MLB will react to the pitch. The pulling G once again attacks across the LOS. The MLB is reacting to the pitch as we expect, and as he generally does, he looks for the backside LB.

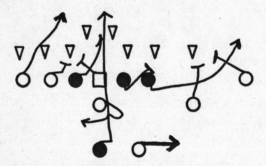

DIAGRAM 4-4

In Diagram 4-5, the blocks by the C and the offside G appear a bit misleading. If the frontside DT closes, he will get trapped by the G. Sometimes the down block by the G will hold the frontside LB, in which case, the C will block him. If it does not hold him, the C will look inside to the offside LB, in which case, the G will bend out to the frontside LB, who might be reacting back to the trap. The type of blocks in the corner made by the receivers will be identical to what we are doing that week in the pitch.

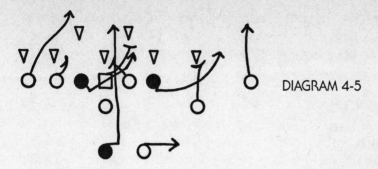

DIAGRAM 4-5

Even though the runner is given a specific point of aim as explained as part of his responsibilities, he may break outside once he clears the LOS, if he reads daylight there. This helps get him away from that backside pursuit.

## PITCH TRAP BOOT

### Play Objective

Since the frontside of the defense must react outside to stop the pitch, it may very well be the backside of the defense that stops the pitch trap. There will probably also be secondary movement to the pitch.

The pitch trap boot will get the defense to think corner attack one side, and then quick counteraction inside. These two fakes, and then a perimeter attack by the QB in the opposite direction, will prove quite effective. At the worst, it will force the defense to play honest.

### Position Responsibilities

*Line*

ONSIDE TACKLE: Works hard at getting good body position by normal onside area run blocking rule and technique.

ONSIDE GUARD: Same as onside tackle.

CENTER: Same as onside tackle.

OFFSIDE GUARD: Pulls behind the center. Attacks the outside breast of the first defender to show outside the block of the onside receiver.

OFFSIDE TACKLE: Fills hard for the pulling guard. Does the same as he would on pitch trap. Does not allow a defender the opportunity to chase or allow penetration.

## Receivers

QUICK END:

*If onside or offside:* Blocks the same as he would on the pitch. He blocks the first man to the inside on or off the line of scrimmage. He does not go inside the normal slot back position. Even if on the offside, this should hold the secondary for a count.

SLOT BACK:

*If onside or offside:* Blocks as in the pitch. He blocks the first man to the inside. He does not go further inside than the normal tackle position on the line of scrimmage. If there is no immediate threat, he seals the LB.

*If in motion to onside:* Attacks the outside breast of the first man to show downfield. He begins on the QB's nod. He should be about 7 or 8 yards ahead of the pulling guard.

*If in motion to offside:* Turns upfield and attacks the first man to show downfield.

STRONG END:

*If onside or offside:* Same as for the quick end.

## Backfield

QUARTERBACK: Fakes the pitch trap. Then he attacks the perimeter. He reads the blocks of the pulling guard as he attacks the outside breast of containment.

QUICK BACK:

*If onside:* Fakes pitch.

*If offside:* Fakes pitch trap. He fills close to the center's butt through the center—pulling guard seam. Remember that the seam will be more onside since the center is blocking onside area run.

STRONG BACK: Same as quick back.

## The Blocking Pattern

### Line

ONSIDE TACKLE: Onside area run.

ONSIDE GUARD: Onside area run.

CENTER: Onside area run.

OFFSIDE GUARD: Pulls and attacks the perimeter.

OFFSIDE TACKLE: Fills.

### Receivers

QUICK END:

*If onside or offside:* Blocks pitch.

SLOT BACK:

*If onside or offside:* Blocks pitch.

*If in motion onside:* Attacks perimeter.

*If in motion offside:* Downfield.

STRONG END: Same as quick end.

### Backfield

QUARTERBACK: Fakes pitch; traps; attacks the perimeter.

QUICK BACK:

*If onside:* Fakes pitch.

*If onside:* Fakes pitch trap.

*If offside:* Fakes pitch trap.

STRONG BACK: Same as quick back.

## Base Play Variations and Looks

See Diagram 4-6 for the pitch trap boot (127 boot) to the strong side. The onside area run blocks for the C, onside G, and onside T will be as explained earlier. Splitting the StE gives a nice crackback effect. This play is a great one for us and has proven effective to either the quick or strong side, with or without motion.

DIAGRAM 4-6

## PITCH TRAP PASS

### Play Objective

With the lateral movement of the linebackers reacting to the pitch and the pitch trap, it will be difficult for them to get a respectable drop once the pass is read. The *pitch trap pass* is geared to take advantage of this.

### Position Responsibilities

*Line*

ONSIDE TACKLE: Pass blocks the first man to show, beginning head up and working outside. If no one is on or outside, he blocks the area.

INSIDE GUARD: Pass blocks the same as the onside tackle.

CENTER: Pass blocks head up, and then works backside away to turn the point of attack. If no one is there to threaten, he blocks the area.

OFFSIDE GUARD: Same as onside guard.

OFFSIDE TACKLE: Same as onside tackle.

*Receivers*

QUICK END:

*If onside:* Fakes inside block, then releases downfield. If open on the seam, he stays on it. If not, he posts at 8 yards.

*If offside:* Fakes inside block, then releases to jet.

SLOT BACK:

*If onside:* Fakes inside block, then releases to jet to outside third. This will force the secondary to cover that zone, and prevent double-covering of the quick end's post.

*If offside:* Pass blocks head up and then outside.

*If in motion to onside:* Immediately gets to outside third on jet.

*If in motion to offside:* Pass blocks the first odd jersey to show outside the tackle's block.

STRONG END:

*If onside:* Same as quick end.

*If offside:* Pass blocks on; outside if aligned tight. If in a split alignment, he fakes inside, then releases to a jet.

*Backfield*

QUARTERBACK: Fakes pitch trap, drops three steps and checks the post. If the post is being overplayed by the safety, the QB pumps and goes deep to the post. If the post is overplayed by the defensive corner, the QB should think jet.

QUICK BACK:

*If onside:* Fakes pitch, then blocks or swings.

*If offside:* Fakes pitch trap in center-guard seam. If tackled, he is doing a good job. If not, once the LB area is cleared, he breaks to flat as secondary receiver.

STRONG BACK:

*If onside or offside:* Same as quick back.

## The Blocking Pattern

*Line*

ONSIDE TACKLE: On, outside, area.

ONSIDE GUARD: On, outside, area.

CENTER: On, outside, area.

OFFSIDE GUARD: On, outside, area.

OFFSIDE TACKLE: On, outside, area.

*Receivers*

QUICK END:

*If onside:* Fake inside, seam, post.

*If offside:* Fake inside, jet.

SLOT BACK:

If onside: Fake inside, jet to outside third.

If offside: On, outside.

If in motion to onside: Jet to outside third.

If in motion to offside: First man outside the tackle.

STRONG END:

If onside: Fake inside, seam, post.

If offside:

Aligned tight: On, outside.

Aligned wide: Fake inside, jet to outside third.

## Backfield

QUARTERBACK: Fakes pitch trap. Thinks post first, then either jet or flat.

QUICK BACK:

If onside: Fakes pitch, block or swing.

If offside: Fakes pitch trap, out to flat.

STRONG BACK:

If onside or offside: Same as quick back.

## Base Play Variations and Looks

Diagram 4-7 shows the pitch trap pass from a slot left with split backs. Note that the line blocks on and then outside, depending on the defensive alignment. The QE will stay on the seam if he is open; otherwise he posts as the primary receiver. The pitch back will block a defender if he shows outside the T's block. If not, he will continue on a swing.

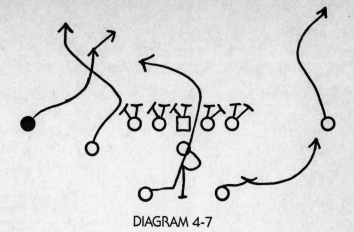

DIAGRAM 4-7

# 5

# Isolating Defenders with Dual Responsibilities

Various plays within the perimeter game offer options to be exercised after the snap of the ball. These are most effective when isolating the typical players within a defensive scheme who have dual responsibilities versus run and pass. These are predominantly the linebackers and the defenders who are responsible for corner support.

The purpose now is to look at those plays that create added pressure for the aforementioned players. Analysis and outline for these plays follow:

> Pitch Read
> Ride Pass
> Dive Keeper
> Lead
> Lead Pass
> Lead Scissors

## ATTACKING PERIMETER PEOPLE WITH DUAL RESPONSIBILITIES

Of the plays listed, the first three (pitch read, ride and pass, and dive keeper) are the ones that specifically tax the containment defenders. By the nature of their run-pass option, they pressure players who have to discern, and then play, both run and pass.

As mentioned in Chapter Three, the *pitch read* attacks the 8 to 10-yard area downfield over the normal slot-quick end alignment. The *ride pass* exploits the reaction of a well-drilled defensive unit to the ride. It puts multiple pressure on the corner with a pass-run option threat. The ride pass is broken down in detail in Chapter Three.

The *dive keeper* attacks the corner in a similar manner as the ride pass. This is discussed completely in Chapter Six. This chapter concentrates on taking advantage of the dual responsibilities assigned to the linebacker in the lead series.

## LEAD

### Play Objective

The *lead* is geared as an attack on a linebacker who has dual run-pass responsibility. It is designed in general to run between the offensive tackles with authority, but it has enough flexibility to adjust the point of attack off-tackle as well. The lead is to the inside game what the pitch is to the outside game.

The lead will get double-teams on the line. Running it from a split backfield allows for the balance of a normal I without the restrictions that the I gives.

In most of the pitch series, the key to executional success is position and lateral offensive movement. Consequently, a "first sound" (set) snap count will facilitate such movement since the offense is still in two-point stances. The lead series stresses explosion and contact, as well as position, as an executional key. The lead attacks areas with gusto that the pitch series hits on misdirection. Most often the snap count is one or two.

### Position Responsibilities

*Line*

ONSIDE TACKLE: If the tackle gives a double-gap call, he will cross block with the onside guard. If he is not double-gapped, he blocks the *defensive tackle*. Note the following definition of a defensive tackle.

## Note: Defensive Tackle Definition

The DT can be anyone on the line of scrimmage from the outside shoulder of the offensive guard to the inside shoulder of the strong end or the slot. It does not matter if the defender is in an up or down stance.

More specifically, the DT would be any defender on the line whom the offensive guard would consider "outside," or whom the strong end or the slot would consider "inside."

ONSIDE GUARD: If the onside tackle gives a double-gap call, the onside guard will cross block with the tackle. If he does not, he will block the defensive guard. Note the following definition of a defensive guard.

## Note: Defensive Guard Definition

The DG can be anyone from head up to the center to the inside shoulder of the offensive tackle. It would be any defender on the line whom the center would call "on" or whom the onside tackle would call "inside."

## Coaching Point on These Definitions

In the area between the onside guard and the onside tackle, a defender might be considered both a defensive guard and a defensive tackle. If such is the case, the defender will be double-teamed, as long as the "cross rule" does not apply.

## Coaching Point on When to Cross Block

When a cross is to take place, the offensive lineman who is to block the man on the line of scrimmage goes first. In the case of two defenders on the line, the blocker who is responsible for the defender closer to the inside goes first.

CENTER: Blocks as normal in the onside area run rule.

OFFSIDE GUARD: Onside area run.

OFFSIDE TACKLE: Onside area run.

## Receivers

### QUICK END:

*If onside or offside:* Bends inside as if to simulate normal perimeter crack. Then he blocks the middle third.

### SLOT BACK:

*If onside:* Blocks the defensive end. The DE is defined as the first man on the line aligned from head up to the slot to his outside. If the point of attack is very tight, he releases to the track.

*If offside:* Attacks the outside third, since the quick end will be taking the middle third.

### STRONG END:

*If onside or offside:* Blocks the same as the slot.

## Backfield

QUARTERBACK: Reverses pivot to about 160 degrees. Reversing too far will force the ballcarrier off his path, unless the point of attack is off-tackle. He makes the handoff and fakes a bootleg fake at the corner.

ONSIDE BACK: Checks the position of the LB, then determines the point of attack. The point of attack will hug the butt of the onside guard versus all defensive sets, except two: (1) if the onside guard-tackle seam is filled, and the off-tackle is open, the point of attack will be just outside of the tackle's butt; and (2) if the onside tackle is double-gapped, the attack will be through the crack of the tackle's butt.

He attacks the near breast of the LB closest to the hole. He expects to find him scraping or filling toward the hole. The back must know the line's blocking pattern for this to be effective.

OFFSIDE BACK: This will be the running back. He must also understand the line's blocking pattern. He determines the point of attack, open steps, and veers hard for the inside hip of the lead back. He should try to be perpendicular to the line of scrimmage by the time he gets to the LOS. This enables him to cut inside or outside.

## The Blocking Pattern

### Line

ONSIDE TACKLE: Crosses with the onside guard if double-gapped. Blocks the DT.

ONSIDE GUARD: Crosses with the onside tackle if the T is double-gapped. Blocks the DG.

CENTER: Onside area run.

OFFSIDE GUARD: Onside area run.

OFFSIDE TACKLE: Onside area run.

### Receivers

QUICK END:

*If onside or offside:* Middle third.

SLOT BACK:

*If onside:* DE, track.

*If offside:* Outside third.

STRONG END:

*If onside or offside:* Same as the slot.

### Backfield

QUARTERBACK: Reverse, handoff, bootleg.

LEAD BACK: Determines POA; attacks near breast of LB.

RUNNING BACK: Determines POA, opens, and veers to inside hip of lead back.

## Base Play Variations and Looks

Diagrams 5-1, 5-2, and 5-3 show a lead left from a slot right (235). It can be run just as easily to either the strong or quick side, with or without motion.

In Diagram 5-1 against a straight Oklahoma, whether the onside G doubles the NG or the DT is a function of the game plan and the opponents' personnel evaluation for that week. However, this assumes that the onside T and the C both give "on" calls. If the T gives an "in" and the C an "on," then the G doubles the DT. If the C gives an "out" and the T an "on," then the G blocks the DT because he is defined as the DG closest to the point of attack. It is *most* important to keep in mind that it is both the blocking pattern plus the communication of the line calls, based on each lineman's interpretation of defensive alignment in his area, that exactly determines who is to be blocked, and exactly determines where the point of attack is.

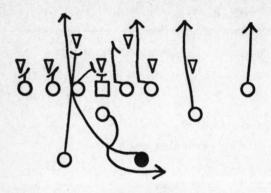

DIAGRAM 5-1

In Diagram 5-2, the onside T will probably give a double-gap call, and, thus, the cross between himself and the onside G. While the offside T may appear on paper to have difficulty reaching in to the offside DT, we have made that block successfully and consistently. However, should the block prove difficult, the offside T can get the help of the offside G with the use of the *seal rule* explained in Chapter Three.

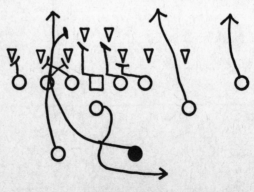

DIAGRAM 5-2

In Diagram 5-3 versus a gap-4, the look should be self-explanatory when looked at in relationship to the blocking pattern.

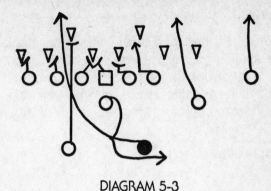

DIAGRAM 5-3

## Statistics for the Lead: Seven Years

The following are the stats accumulated for the lead over seven years at two very different schools. Please keep in mind that the programs at both schools began as major rebuilding situations.

| AT SCHOOL I | | | | | | |
|---|---|---|---|---|---|---|
| SEASON | GAMES | NO. RUN | TOTAL YARDS | AVG. GAIN | NEG. YARDS NO. PLAYS | LOST FUMBLES |
| SEASON I (4-5-0) | 9 | 38 | 148 | 3.9 | 3 | 2 |
| SEASON II (5-3-1) | 9 | 50 | 220 | 4.4 | 2 | 0 |
| SEASON III (8-1-0) | 9 | 62 | 329 | 5.3 | 0 | 1 |
| SEASON IV (8-1-0) | 9 | 70 | 364 | 5.2 | 1 | 0 |
| AT SCHOOL II | | | | | | |
| SEASON I (1-8-1) | 10 | 65 | 260 | 4.0 | 1 | 1 |
| SEASON II (3-7-0) | 10 | 62 | 267 | 4.3 | 1 | 2 |
| SEASON III (6-4-1) | 11 | 72 | 367 | 5.1 | 0 | 1 |

## LEAD PASS

### Play Objective

In order to stop the lead, it is necessary for the LB to fill the POA hard. The initial look of the *lead pass,* which is identical to the *lead, scissors,* and *boot,* forces the LB to begin such action. This will prevent him from getting to his normal area of responsibility, which is the hook-curl areas in most zone coverages.

### Position Responsibilities

#### Line

ONSIDE TACKLE: Aggressively blocks anyone considered "on." If there is no one "on," he blocks the first man to show to the outside. He must remember to keep himself between the QB and the defender, and remember also that the QB's action will have him setting up to the offside.

Note that the onside in this case is the side to which the fake is being run.

ONSIDE GUARD: Pulls behind the center and attacks the first man to show outside the offside tackle's block. He works for the outside breast position on the defender.

CENTER: Makes area pass away from the fake, but does not wheel.

OFFSIDE GUARD: Makes area pass outside. He must remember that the QB will be setting to his side.

OFFSIDE TACKLE: Same as offside guard.

#### Receivers

QUICK END:

*If fake is to his side:* The QE initially runs the pattern the same as he would if blocking the lead in the middle third. As he drives toward the middle third, he finds the open area between the middle third where the strong end has taken the safety deep, and the hook-curl zones where the lead fake has prevented a quick drop by the linebackers. He works for a depth of about 15 yards.

*If fake is to other side:* Again, he runs the same route that he would if he were blocking the lead in the middle third. This time, he takes the safety deep.

SLOT BACK:

*If fake is to his side:* Blocks the first defender to show outside the tackle's block. If there is no rush, he releases hard to the outside third.

*If fake is to other side:* Follows the route of the quick end looking for the open area between the middle third and the hook-curl areas. He works for a depth of about 15 yards.

STRONG END:

*If fake is to his side:* Does the same as the slot when the fake is to his side.

*If fake is to other side:* Attacks the middle third; takes the safety deep. This is similar to the technique of the quick end when the fake is to the other side of the quick end.

## Backfield

QUARTERBACK: He will tight reverse pivot, since the fake back will fill in the G-T seam. He begins boot fake, but gains depth in the process. He sets behind the G-T seam at a depth of about 5 yards. He looks to the intermediate area between the middle third and the hook-curl zones first. The deep middle third will generally be the secondary receivers.

LEAD BACK: Fills for the pulling guard as close to the center's butt as possible. If there is no threat, he continues on route and releases immediately to the flat to the side to which the QB is setting. As he gets to the flat area, he turns it up. He does not go deeper than 8 yards before turning it up.

FAKE BACK: Fakes lead handoff, then fills for the pulling guard just outside the lead back. If there is no threat, he runs a route similar to the lead back, but to the side of the fake.

## The Blocking Pattern

### Line

ONSIDE TACKLE: Passes block on, outside.

ONSIDE GUARD: Pulls opposite to containment.

CENTER: Outside areas pass away from the fake.

OFFSIDE GUARD: Outside area pass.

OFFSIDE TACKLE: Outside area pass.

### Receivers

QUICK END:

*If onside to fake:* Finds open area in intermediate middle third.

*If offside to fake:* Drives to the deep middle third.

SLOT BACK:

*If onside to fake:* Blocks DE, releases to outside intermediate third.

*If offside to fake:* Finds open area in intermediate middle third.

STRONG END:

*If onside to fake:* Blocks DE, releases to outside intermediate third.

*If offside to fake:* Drives to deep middle third.

### Backfield

QUARTERBACK: He will reverse, boot behind G-T seam, and check intermediate middle third as primary route.

LEAD BACK: Fills next to center, swings to flat and up.

FAKE BACK: Fakes lead, fills next to lead back, swings to flat and up.

## Coaching Notes on Play Variations

### Lead pass deep

This will be run exactly like the lead pass, except the primary route will be either the quick end or the strong end on his drive in the deep middle third.

### Lead pass Sam

This will be run exactly the same as the lead pass, except the slot in the intermediate outside third will be the secondary receiver. Since the DE may be rushing, it will still be necessary to check the intermediate middle third first. Note that this play must be run with the fake to the side of the *slot.*

### Lead pass swing

Again, while the play will be run exactly like the lead pass, the secondary receiver will be the halfbacks on their swing routes. The intermediate middle third must still be considered primary since the backs may be forced to block.

## Base Play Variations and Looks

In Diagrams 5-4 and 5-5 the lead pass is run both to the strong and the quick sides. Note the T, to the side of the fake, blocks either on or outside, depending on the defensive look in his zone. The C, offside G, and T execute an onside area pass technique to the outside. In both cases the middle curl is the primary receiver. In both cases the StE or the SB to the side of the fake will block first; while the fake back is expected to get tackled, the lead back should be able to get into the pattern.

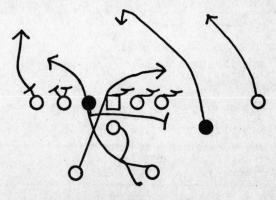

DIAGRAM 5-4

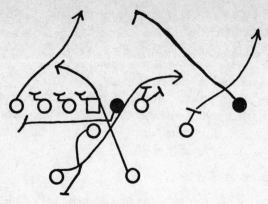

DIAGRAM 5-5

## SCISSORS

### Play Objective

The function of this play is to have complete misdirection action. Since the lead is a quick, explosive hitter, the well-executed misdirection off it has proven most effective. The scissors is to the lead as the reverse is to the pitch.

Since the slot is carrying the ball, it can be run only to the strong end side.

### Position Responsibilities

*Line*

QUICK TACKLE: Fills aggressively for the pulling guard, then gets to the track.

QUICK GUARD: Pulls behind the center and kicks out the first man to show outside the strong end's block.

CENTER: Blocks on first. If no one is there, he blocks the onside area run.

STRONG GUARD: Same as center.

STRONG TACKLE: Same as center.

*Receivers*

QUICK END: Blocks the middle third.

SLOT BACK: Releases inside parallel to the line of scrimmage. As opposed to the reverse, he must keep in mind that the

QB will be on the strong side after the lead fake. The SB will pass between the QB, who will open to him and the line of scrimmage. The SB hugs the strong end's block as the SB veers to the off-tackle hole.

STRONG END: Blocks the first man to show to the inside, regardless of whether he is on or off the line. Keeps outside leverage.

### Backfield

QUARTERBACK: Reverses pivot as in the lead, but continues to come around on almost a 360-degree pivot. The exact degree turn of this pivot will depend on the timing between the QB and the SB. The pivot, however, should move in unison with the movement of the fake back. He makes the handoff to the slot back and attacks the corner to the quick side.

QUICK BACK: Fills the center-onside guard seam, hugging the center's butt. If there is no threat, he goes to the track.

STRONG BACK: Open steps, fakes lead handoff, and fills area outside the quick tackle. He must remember that the quick tackle is blocking down and be sure not to get in the way of the path of the slot back.

## The Blocking Pattern

### Line

QUICK TACKLE: Fills for guard; tracks.

QUICK GUARD: Pulls opposite, kicks out containment.

CENTER: On, onside area run.

STRONG GUARD: Same as center.

STRONG TACKLE: Same as center.

### Receivers

QUICK END: Middle third.

SLOT BACK: Releases parallel to LOS, takes handoff and veers off-tackle.

STRONG END: First man inside.

*Backfield*

QUARTERBACK: Reverses to a 360-degree pivot with depth handoff; attacks quick side.

QUICK BACK: Fills for pulling G, hugs center.

STRONG BACK: Fakes lead; fills outside onside tackle.

## Base Play and Look

Diagram 5-6 shows the scissors (134) versus a base fifty. If the StE reads that the StT has the DT by himself, he will slide off to the LB. With the lead back filling in the C-G seam, backside pursuit on the LOS has proven ineffective.

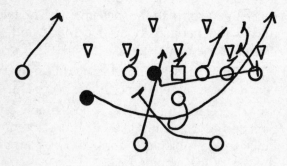

DIAGRAM 5-6

## Note on Motion

For the most part, *motion* was not discussed in this chapter. In the lead, motion would predominantly be used as a decoy. The only caution here is to make sure that when running the lead to the quick side with motion away, the normal defensive end will not be a factor in hurting the offensive play. Note also that if the DE tightens after motion begins, the tackle may be faced with a double-gap look. If the quick tackle doesn't anticipate this before motion takes place, it may be too late to make the call. For example, look at the situation versus a wide-tackle in Diagrams 5-7 and 5-8.

While motion can certainly be incorporated in the lead pass, I would question whether or not it is worth the time. If motion is a big part of your attack, it would prove an effective perimeter route to the strong side off a quickside fake. The only difficulty might be a backside rush, which could perhaps be picked up by the fake back. See Diagram 5-9. Whether or not this is really worth your time depends upon your individual offense and philosophy.

In the scissors, putting the slot in motion would be necessary, if the slot is consistently split wide. This then would be imperative for timing. If the slot is split between 1 and 3 yards, motion would probably hurt the timing.

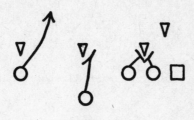

DIAGRAM 5-7

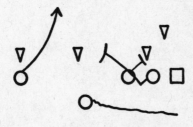

DIAGRAM 5-8

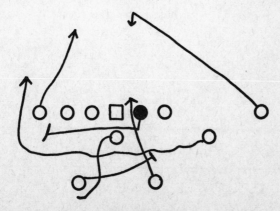

DIAGRAM 5-9

# 6

# Blasting the Defensive Interior

No offensive scheme can be sound unless its running game can attack three areas: inside, off-tackle, and outside. The Perimeter Attack Offense must also utilize this principle if it is to be sound.

This chapter provides an analysis of not only how the power and dive series blast away at the interior, but also how they complement the perimeter and play action games.

The same principles of *isolation* that are discussed in Chapter Five regarding the lead series are also an intricate part of both of these series.

From the *power series*, we will look at:

> Power
> Power Pass
> Power Pitch

From the *dive series*, we will deal with:

> Dive
> Dive Pop
> Dive Keeper

## POWER

### Play Objective

The principles behind the *power* are really the same as they are in the *lead,* except the formation is run from a power backfield set. The wishbone type of alignment is not meant to pose as a triple option attack, but instead, as a perfectly balanced Power-I. The power will also attack a linebacker who has dual responsibilities, but it does so with two lead backs. The entire power series has proven to be an outstanding goal-line offense.

### Position Responsibilities

#### Line

All responsibilities here are exactly the same as they are in the lead.

#### Receivers

All responsibilities here are exactly the same as they are in the lead. Remember that now you are dealing with only a strong end and quick end. The slot has moved to the backfield as a fullback.

#### Backfield

QUARTERBACK: His initial movement and handoff is the same as it is in the lead. He reverses to about 160 degrees, makes the handoff, and then attacks the corner in the same direction as the power. This is different in the lead, where the QB bootlegs opposite the play.

FULLBACK: Of course, a change in personnel may be necessary here. He determines the point of attack the same way the lead back would in the lead.

However, if the play is geared to hit off-tackle, the fullback will hit the first open seam to the onside. He will begin with the C-G seam first.

He will attack the playside breast of the first man to show. If his movement is to the G-T seam and the play is to be run inside, he will take a short playside lateral step before attacking the defense. This puts the fullback in a better blocking relationship with the lead back.

LEAD BACK: Exactly the same as in the lead, except he must be more conscious of the blocking relationship between the FB and the lead back. When both the FB and the lead back are going through the same hole, he attacks the inside breast of the first man to show from the outside.

RUNNING BACK: Exactly the same as in the lead. He runs to the inside hip of the lead back. He keeps in mind all the coaching points stressed in the lead.

## The Blocking Pattern

*Line*

Same as for the lead.

*Receivers*

Same as for the lead.

*Backfield*

QUARTERBACK: Reverses, makes handoff, rolls attack to corner.

FULLBACK: Attacks first man to show at the POA. If POA is off-tackle, he hits the first vacant seam inside.

LEAD BACK: Same as the lead.

RUNNING BACK: Same as the lead.

## Coaching Point on Leg Movement

Probably the most important coaching point for a play like this is the constant movement of all offensive legs, especially the ones in and around the hole.

When *both* offensive and defensive execution is good, there is seldom a clean tackle of the ballcarrier. Instead, there is generally a clog or pileup at the point of attack. It is imperative that no "leaning" takes place in or around the hole. That constant leg movement will mean a good extra 2 yards in the end result.

## Base Play and Looks

Make note of Diagram 6-1 for a power right from a power left alignment (556). All the blocking is the movement of the fullback.

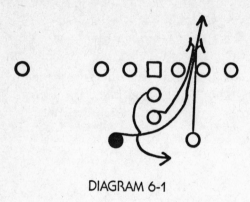

DIAGRAM 6-1

## POWER PASS

### Play Objective

With the force that the power hits inside, it is quite important that the defensive end or the outside linebacker keeps his inside seam squeezed as tight as possible. If the defender does not do this, he allows too much room inside to execute the power.

With all the activity going on to his inside, there is a tendency by many defenders to turn inside. Even those who stay parallel to the line tend to become preoccupied with all the inside action. This point can be argued on paper, but the fact remains that the power has had this effect over the years on the DE or the OLB. There is a definite tendency for that defender to become complacent to the roll fake of the QB as he concentrates his attention inside. This allows the QB to attack the corner in a run-pass option.

### Position Responsibilities

*Line*

Exactly the same as in the power, but no one should go downfield. The key here is to make the corner attack look identical to the inside run.

### Receivers

QUICK END:

*If onside:* Runs a quick post to the middle third. Makes the break at 5 yards. This depth will vary in goal-line situations.

*If offside:* Runs a *deep seam* between the middle and outside thirds.

STRONG END:

*If onside:* Begins to block the defensive end or outside linebacker. He holds for a 2 count, then releases on a bend to the flat. He works to a depth of about 10 yards. He turns upfield on the QB's pump.

*If offside:* Runs a deep seam between the middle and outside thirds.

### Backfield

QUARTERBACK:

Fakes the power handoff. Attacks the corner in the same direction as the fake, and gets parallel to the line of scrimmage at a depth of about 5 to 7 yards. He should think run first, but look to the bend area for the pass. Unless the receivers are wide open, he throws the ball on the run in order to keep the pressure on the corner.

FULLBACK:

Fakes the power. If there is no opposition as there should be at the line, he gets to a middle hook of about 8 yards and waves to the QB. This may tighten the safety and open the deep middle third.

LEAD BACK:

Fakes the power. If to the quick side, he does a short bend seam between the middle and outside thirds.

FAKE BACK:

Fakes the power. He stays low and keeps moving; if he isn't, he runs into the nearest defensive lineman.

## The Blocking Pattern

### Line

Same as the power, but no downfield.

*Receivers*

QUICK END:

> *If onside:* quick post.

> *If offside:* Deep seam.

STRONG END:

> *If onside:* Delay block and bend.

> *If offside:* Deep seam.

*Backfield*

QUARTERBACK: Fakes power, rolls attack play side.

FULLBACK: Fakes power, decoys to short middle hook.

LEAD BACK:

> *If to quick side:* short bend.

> *If to strong side:* deep seam.

FAKE BACK: Fakes power.

## Play Variation: Power Pass Deep

This is run exactly like the power pass except the quarterback will pull up behind the fakeside tackle and will gain more depth behind the line. He will then look to the backside deep seam route as his primary receiver. If the defensive secondary is not disciplined, this will be a score or a big gainer.

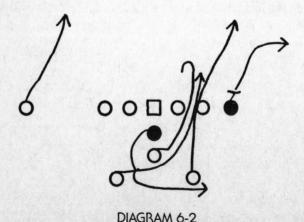

DIAGRAM 6-2

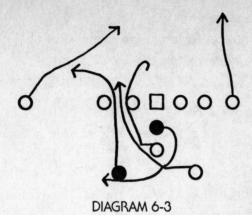

DIAGRAM 6-3

## Base Play and Looks

See Diagrams 6-2 and 6-3 for the power pass to both the strong and the quick side. To the strong side, the StE is the primary receiver, as is the QkB to the quick side. In both cases, however, the QB will have a run-first option, unless he is a superior passer. If power pass deep is called, then the QB thinks *pass* first.

## POWER PITCH

### Play Objective

This play is run almost completely identical to the pitch. The theory is that we want to be able to run our best play from a totally different formation. An element of surprise here would just make the pitch that much more effective.

### Position Responsibilities

*Line*

All the responsibilities for the line are exactly the same as they are in the pitch.

*Receivers*

QUICK END:

> *If onside:* Inside.
> *If offside:* Middle third.

STRONG END:

> *If onside:* Reach inside, seal inside.

> *If offside:* Middle third.

### Backfield

QUARTERBACK: Same as the pitch.

FULLBACK: Same as the quick or strong back when he is offside.

QUICK BACK:

> *If onside or offside:* Same as the pitch.

STRONG BACK:

> *If onside or offside:* Same as the pitch.

## Base Play and Look

See Diagram 6-4 for a 652, the power pitch from a power right formation.

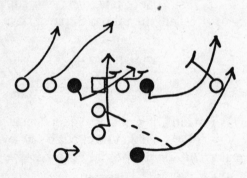

DIAGRAM 6-4

## MOTION IN THE POWER SERIES

Motion adds a nice feature in a series, and would specifically be executed by the fullback. It should be relatively easy to visualize how FB motion can be an asset to the power pitch. The FB can be used either as an extra lead blocker with the pulling tackle on the corner, or as a wide receiver who is used to crackback inside to seal off pursuit.

Also note that when the FB does go into motion, what remains is the normal splitback alignment. From that alignment, the entire lead series can then be run. If this is the case, the FB is used primarily as a decoy.

Remember from Chapter One that FB motion is called "fly" in the huddle.

## SEVEN-YEAR STATISTICS FOR THE POWER

The following are the stats at both schools over the seven years. Keep in mind that both programs began as major rebuilding situations.

| AT SCHOOL I | | | | | | |
|---|---|---|---|---|---|---|
| SEASON | GAMES | NO. RUN | TOTAL YARDS | AVG. GAIN | NEG. YARDS NO. PLAYS | LOST FUMBLES |
| SEASON I (4-5-0) | 9 | 48 | 163 | 3.4 | 2 | 3 |
| SEASON II (5-3-1) | 9 | 37 | 144 | 3.9 | 0 | 1 |
| SEASON III (8-1-0) | 9 | 30 | 132 | 4.4 | 1 | 0 |
| SEASON IV (8-1-0) | 9 | 34 | 146 | 4.3 | 0 | 1 |
| AT SCHOOL II | | | | | | |
| SEASON I (1-8-1) | 10 | 38 | 137 | 3.6 | 2 | 1 |
| SEASON II (3-7-0) | 10 | 44 | 176 | 4.0 | 2 | 0 |
| SEASON III (6-4-1) | 11 | 45 | 194 | 4.3 | 1 | 0 |

## DIVE

### Play Objective

The design here is to also attack the defenders with a dual responsibility. What is given up in the dive, as opposed to the lead and power, is the double-teams on the line of scrimmage at the point of attack, and the effect of the lead back(s). The advantage is the quickness with which the dive hits. The Dive Series can be run from any one of the normal offensive formations where two set backs remain.

## Position Responsibilities

### Line

ONSIDE TACKLE: He is the first man to show beginning in a head-up position. If no one is there, he blocks the first man on the line to the outside. If no one is there, he blocks the LB. He crosses with the G on "double gaps."

INSIDE GUARD: Blocks on, outside, LB as the onside tackle does. He crosses with the T on "double gaps" around the T.

CENTER: Blocks on, up, LB.

OFFSIDE GUARD: Same as the center.

OFFSIDE TACKLE: Gets to the track.

### Receivers

OFFSIDE END: Middle third.

ONSIDE END: Blocks the man responsible for playing the onside outside third.

OFFSIDE END: Blocks the man responsible for playing the offside outside third.

SLOT BACK: Blocks the middle third.

### Backfield

QUARTERBACK: The first step should be a large open step to about 90 degrees. The second step should cross the other foot over. The third step brings the QB up to the ballcarrier. He makes the handoff, then gets on the outside hip of the offside back, who is attacking the frontside corner.

ONSIDE BACK: This is the running back. His point of aim should always be the inside leg of the onside tackle. This facilitates the timing between himself and the quarterback. As the handoff is made, he then veers to the proper point of attack. He should still be hitting the hole at a perpendicular as he gets to the line of scrimmage. The POA will be the same for him as it is in the lead. Consequently, this could look like both the inside and the outside veer defending on the defensive alignment.

OFFSIDE BACK: Takes off at top speed to the playside sideline. He keeps his depth and stays parallel to the line of scrimmage. He attacks the outside breast of the first man to show outside the tackle's block, or outside the guard's block if the tackle gives a double-gap call.

## The Blocking Pattern

### Line

ONSIDE TACKLE: If "double gaps," he crosses with the guard. On, outside, LB.

ONSIDE GUARD: If tackle gives "double gaps," he will cross. On, outside, LB.

CENTER: On, up, LB.

OFFSIDE GUARD: On, up, LB.

OFFSIDE TACKLE: Track.

### Receivers

ONSIDE END: Onside outside third.

OFFSIDE END: Offside outside third.

SLOT BACK: Middle third.

### Backfield

QUARTERBACK: Opens, gives handoff, attacks corner.

ONSIDE BACK: His point of aim is the inside leg of the tackle. He determines to the point of attack and takes the handoff.

OFFSIDE BACK: Attacks the playside perimeter.

## Base Play Look

In Diagram 6-5, a dive right is being run from a slot right (246) against a fifty with an *eagle* adjustment to the offense's quick side.

Should the split of the SB be relatively tight, the DE might affect the play. If that's the case, the onside T will make a double-gap call, and then he and the onside G will cross. As in the *lead*, the point of attack for the dive back is off-T, since the G-T seam is filled and the off-tackle is vacant. However, the dive back's point of aim initially is the inside leg of the T. If the G is driving the DT toward the POA, as may happen here, the back should cut inside that block.

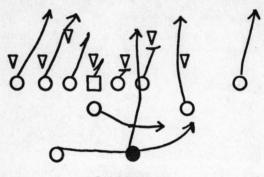

DIAGRAM 6-5

In Diagram 6-6, the play (245) is being run to the strong side versus a split-4. The point of attack on the double-gap call becomes the butt of the T on alignment. The offside G and the offside T can go to a "seal" call if the onside DT poses a problem. However, with the quick-hitting nature of the play, this has not proven a problem. This quick-hitter inside also poses a nice change of pace for the offense and gives the defense something to prepare for.

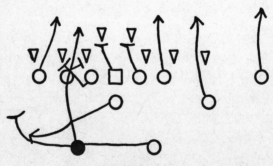

DIAGRAM 6-6

## DIVE POP

### Play Objective

As in the case of the lead pass, the objective here is to hold the linebacker on the fake. This should make it difficult to get back to his normal hook-curl area in most zone coverages.

### Position Responsibilities

*Line*

ONSIDE TACKLE: Aggressively blocks the onside area pass to the outside.

ONSIDE GUARD: Aggressively blocks on, onside area pass.

CENTER: Blocks offside area pass. He must remember that the offside area pass is blocked the same as the onside area pass, except the initial step of the blocker goes offside rather than onside. A defender who is head up will get blocked. He must be aggressive to simulate run.

OFFSIDE GUARD: Same as the center.

OFFSIDE TACKLE: Same as the center.

*Receivers*

QUICK END:

*If onside:* Quick post at 5 yards.

*If offside:* Deep seam.

SLOT BACK:

*If onside:* Quick out at 5 yards. The objective here is to keep the cornerback outside, so he can't squeeze the quick end inside.

*If offside:* Drives to middle third. Takes the safety deep.

STRONG END:

*If onside:* Short or intermediate seam. It is all right to bend to the middle hook area at about 10 yards.

*If offside:* Drives to middle third. Takes safety deep.

## Backfield

QUARTERBACK: Fakes dive handoff. He must remember that this is to be a healthy ride fake, not a quick job or hand fake. It is this "ride" action that will hold the linebackers. After the fake, he gives the impression that he is attacking the corner as he gains his depth. He pulls up behind the frontside tackle at a depth of 5 yards. He will need to take only two or three steps.

He tries to "pop" the ball to the end on the quick post or the short seam, depending on which side the play is to go. If the end is covered, the QB goes to the deep middle third.

ONSIDE BACK: This is the fake back. He takes a point of aim between the C and the onside G. If that seam is occupied by a defender, he expects a collision—he *initiates* that collision! If that hole is vacant, he veers to the LB. If he isn't tackled, he runs an out to the flat and up.

OFFSIDE BACK: Exactly like the dive.

# The Blocking Pattern

## Line

ONSIDE TACKLE: Onside area pass to the outside.

ONSIDE GUARD: On, onside area pass.

CENTER: Offside area pass.

OFFSIDE GUARD: Offside area pass.

OFFSIDE TACKLE: Offside area pass.

## Receivers

QUICK END:

*If onside:* Quick post at 5.

*If offside:* Middle third.

SLOT BACK:

*If onside:* Quick out at 5.

*If offside:* Middle third.

SLOT END:

> *If onside:* Short or intermediate seam.
>
> *If offside:* Middle third.

## Backfield

QUARTERBACK: Fakes dive, pulls up behind tackle. He thinks "pop" to quick post or short seam.

ONSIDE BACK: Fakes dive, bends and up.

OFFSIDE BACK: Dive.

## Base Play Looks

See Diagram 6-7 for a (145) pop. Unless the C-G seam is filled, the back will run directly at the LB after a good ride fake, thereby opening the "throwing lane" for the quick post by the QE.

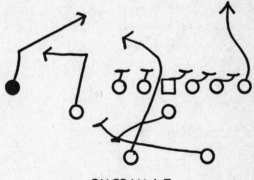

DIAGRAM 6-7

## DIVE KEEPER

## Play Objective

The key here is to simulate that hard, quick-hitting dive inside, crack block on the corner with the receivers, and attack outside fast and furious. If the inside game has been effective, pursuit from the defense will not be strong. The consequence will be an effective perimeter attack once again.

## Position Responsibilities

### Line

The entire line blocks the onside area run, except for the offside tackle, who tracks.

### Receivers

All blocking rules for the *pitch* are executed now for all three receivers.

### Backfield

QUARTERBACK: Gives a good dive fake, then gets on the outside hip of the offside back and attacks the perimeter.

ONSIDE BACK: Takes the same point as usual on the dive. However, once the fake is made, he veers off-tackle automatically. This *outside veer* effect could hold the defenders closer to the perimeter, thereby making the QB's attack on the corner more effective.

OFFSIDE BACK: Attacks that perimeter!

## The Blocking Pattern

### Line

Same as the position responsibilities.

### Receivers

Same as the pitch.

### Backfield

QUARTERBACK: Fakes dive, attacks the perimeter.

ONSIDE BACK: Veers off-tackle.

OFFSIDE BACK: Attacks the perimeter.

## Base Play Look

Diagram 6-8 shows the dive keeper to the strong side with the StE split to take advantage of the crackback. The StE, however, could just as easily be tight, and the play would still be effective. The QB will get on the outside lip of the offside back and read the perimeter just as the running back does with the pulling tackle on the pitch.

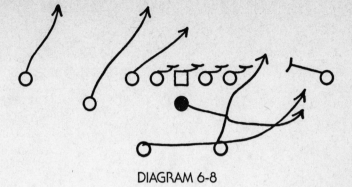

DIAGRAM 6-8

# 7

# Bootlegging It
# to the Corner

There is tremendous pressure placed on the corner when the offense can attack it off the snap of the ball. However, to do that after a play has been faked in an opposite direction can be devastating. This is really the entire objective of *bootleg* action.

The following plays will be discussed in this chapter:

Boot
Boot Pass
Pitch Trap Boot
Reverse Pass
Lead Around

The boot and the boot pass at one time were practically one play. The boot, in actuality, was the boot pass. There was no boot, as will be explained later. The boot was a run-pass option.

On occasion, it was necessary to predetermine that the quarterback would run and lose the pass part of his option. Tendency and game situation dictated this. The irony, however, was the amazing success of the predetermined run, especially when you keep in mind that the real pressure on the defense generally came from executing a run-pass threat.

The result was that by the third year at my first school, the predetermined run became the *boot,* and the boot became the *boot pass.* It became the big gainer in the offense, although it is not used nearly so often as the lead or the pitch. A detailed analysis of both plays follow in this chapter.

The pitch trap boot and reverse pass are outlined in Chapter Four. The pitch trap boot, also a predetermined run, has also enjoyed great success. Since it comes off not just the pitch, but the pitch trap, there are two complete fakes that have to be executed before the boot is carried out. Also, the QB is actually on the side of the center, opposite the boot, when he begins his attack on the corner. The normal boot comes off the lead. The QB is already on the side of his boot attack and the lead fake is much quicker. Consequently, the pitch trap boot gets used less frequently.

The *reverse pass* could just as easily be called the *reverse boot pass.* In fact, at one time it was. The reverse comes off the pitch. The QB fakes the reverse, then pulls up to pass as he begins his attack on the corner. This is really a pass first, run second option. Seldom does the run have to be executed.

While I felt it fitting that both the reverse pass and pitch trap boot plays be mentioned here, there will be no further analysis other than what has been explained in Chapter Four.

The lead around, along with its play variations, *give lead around* and *lead around pass,* are really not bootlegs. They are appropriate to analyze in this chapter, though, because they come off the lead and provide a form of misdirection in a corner attack. The difference between this and the bootlegs are (1) the QB does not keep the ball, and (2) the misdirection of the point of attack takes place to the same side of the inside fake. In the boots, the QB keeps the ball and attacks the corner opposite his last fake.

## BOOT

### Play Objective

The lead is geared at attacking the interior of the defense with quick-hitting isolation action. It is stopped by a quick, hard fill by the linebacker at the point of attack, and by good, hard, aggressive play.

By faking that same play inside, pursuit to the corner is effected. The receivers, to the side of boot action, treat their responsibilities as they do the pitch. The effect of pitch blocking on the corner, and the absence of quality inside-out pursuit off a run fake in the opposite direction, can make this play *the* game breaker in the offense, as long as the quarterback has respectable speed and running ability.

## Position Responsibilities

### Line

ONSIDE TACKLE: This is the tackle to whom the side of the boot is run. He blocks the onside area run.

ONSIDE GUARD: Same as the onside tackle.

CENTER: Same as the onside tackle.

OFFSIDE GUARD: This is the guard on whose side the lead is faked to. He pulls behind the center, turns upfield outside the block of the receivers, and attacks the outside breast of the first man to show on the corner.

OFFSIDE TACKLE: Blocks the defensive tackle as he would in the lead, then releases downfield to the track.

### Receivers

All receivers block the same way as they do in the pitch if they are onside. If they are offside, they get downfield to block their respective thirds.

### Backfield

QUARTERBACK: Begins with a good long fake for the lead. As the ball gets to his offside hip, he pulls it and begins his attack on the corner. He must remember that on this fake (as in the lead), his back is to be parallel to the line of scrimmage. As he attacks the corner, his relationship with the pulling guard should be similar to the back and the tackle in the pitch. He works at staying on the pulling guard's outside hip.

OFFSIDE BACK: This is the back who normally is the lead back in the lead. He fills as tightly to the center as possible. He must remember that the center is blocking the onside area run, and that he will be moving away from him. This tight fill is necessary in order to pick up any defensive front stunts.

ONSIDE BACK: This is the back who is the running back in the lead. After the lead fake, he fills tightly off the butt of the lead back. The effect here is that both the center-pulling guard seam and the pulling guard-offside tackle seam are both taken care of.

## The Blocking Pattern

### Line

ONSIDE TACKLE: Onside area run.

ONSIDE GUARD: Onside area run.

CENTER: Onside area run.

OFFSIDE GUARD: Pulls and attacks the perimeter.

OFFSIDE TACKLE: DT, track.

### Receivers

IF ONSIDE: Same as the pitch.

IF OFFSIDE: Their respective thirds.

### Backfield

QUARTERBACK: Fakes lead and attacks the perimeter.

OFFSIDE BACK: Fills next to the center.

ONSIDE BACK: Fakes lead, fills next to the lead back.

## Play Look

See Diagram 7-1 for the boot being run to the slot (235 boot). The C, onside G, and onside T block the normal onside area run.

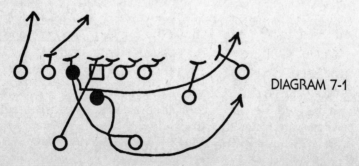

DIAGRAM 7-1

The backside T blocks the DT as he does in the lead, and then gets to the track. The exact blocking by the receivers will depend on how the pitch is blocked in the corner that week. As is true throughout the entire offense, the fake is a good, long ride by the QB, who then gets in the outside hip of the pulling G.

## Boot Statistics

Once again, these are stats at two very different schools over major rebuilding situations.

| SEASON | GAMES | NO. RUN | TOTAL YARDS | AVG. GAIN | NEG. YARDS NO. PLAYS | LOST FUMBLES |
|---|---|---|---|---|---|---|
| AT SCHOOL I | | | | | | |
| SEASON I | | | | | | |
| SEASON II | *Note:* This play in the above analyzed form was not used until the third season. | | | | | |
| SEASON III | 9 | 24 | 173 | 7.2 | 3 | 0 |
| SEASON IV | 9 | 29 | 229 | 7.9 | 4 | 0 |
| AT SCHOOL II | | | | | | |
| SEASON I | 10 | 34 | 201 | 5.9 | 6 | 1 |
| SEASON II | 10 | 32 | 205 | 6.4 | 6 | 0 |
| SEASON III | 11 | 33 | 248 | 7.5 | 5 | 0 |

## BOOT PASS

### Play Objective

The boot pass is again geared as a run-pass option on the corner. The key to success here is the *boot* action. Most of the passing from the pitch and the power series come off *"roll"* action. This is action where the QB attacks the corner in the same direction as his initial fake.

The objective is to get the secondaries to begin movement in one direction and then attack the perimeter in the other. It is also aimed at holding the linebackers up front as they play the run.

## Position Responsibilities

### Line

ONSIDE TACKLE: Blocks onside area pass, but does not use the wheel technique. This might just get in the way of the quarterback and his attack to the corner.

ONSIDE GUARD: Blocks the same as the onside tackle.

CENTER: Blocks the same as the onside tackle.

OFFSIDE GUARD: Pulls behind the center and attacks the first man to show on the corner. He expects a quick rush by the defensive end or the outside linebacker. If there is none, he continues the attack on the corner, but he does not go downfield unless the QB gives a "go" call.

OFFSIDE TACKLE: Pass blocks the defensive tackle and keeps himself between the DT and the QB.

### Receivers

QUICK END:

*If onside:* Reads the coverage in the outside third. If he can beat it, he runs deep. If he can't, he runs a comeback from 18 to 16 yards.

*If offside:* Runs a crossing route to a depth of 12 to 14 yards, reading the coverage of the linebackers.

STRONG END:

*If onside:* Same as the quick end when the quick end is onside.

*If offside:* Same as the slot back when the slot is offside.

### Backfield

QUARTERBACK: Fakes the lead and begins the perimeter attack. As soon as the lead is faked, the QB trains his eyes to focus on the perimeter patterns. He does not go too deep to belly around a defender trying to contain, if that containment comes immediately. If such is the case, the QB pulls up and reads the perimeter coverage. If covered, he looks to the backside cross.

If containment does not happen immediately, he continues the attack on the corner and reads the perimeter coverage. If covered, he can either (1) give a "go" call and run, or (2) check the backside cross. If the cross is covered, he gives a "go" call and runs.

Whether the QB executes choice 1 or choice 2 will be determined by the type of player the QB is.

OFFSIDE BACK: Fills next to the center as in the lead. If there is any threat of penetration, he blocks it. If there isn't, he continues to the onside flat at a depth of about 4 yards as the safety valve

OFFSIDE BACK: Fills next to the lead back as in the lead. Picks up any threat.

## The Blocking Pattern

### Line

ONSIDE TACKLE: Onside area pass.

ONSIDE GUARD: Onside area pass.

CENTER: Onside area pass.

OFFSIDE GUARD: Pulls and attacks the perimeter.

OFFSIDE TACKLE: DT.

### Receivers

QUICK END:

*If onside:* Reads coverage. Deep or comeback.

*If offside:* Post.

SLOT BACK:

*If onside:* Out.

*If offside:* Cross.

STRONG END:

*If onside:* Read coverage. Deep or comeback.

*If offside:* Cross.

### Backfield

QUARTERBACK: Fakes lead and attacks the perimeter. Reads perimeter coverage first, then does "go" or cross.

OFFSIDE BACK: Fakes lead. Flat.

ONSIDE BACK: Fakes lead.

## Play look

Diagram 7-2 shows the boot pass to the slot (235 boot pass). Should the QE read that he is covered deep, there will be a flood effect to the side of the QB's attack. The QB will look to the crossing pattern or run off a "go" call if the perimeter coverage covers the perimeter pattern.

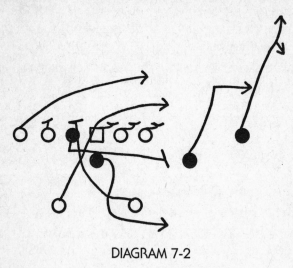

DIAGRAM 7-2

## LEAD AROUND

## Play Objective

The function here is to get lead action one side and then go to the slot off reverse movement. A necessary ingredient in any type of reverse perimeter play is *speed*. If the normal slot does not have good speed, it may be necessary to substitute for him. If there is no speed at that position at all, then it may be wise not to run the play.

## Position Responsibilities

### Line

ONSIDE TACKLE: This is the tackle to the "around" side, which is opposite the lead. Block aggressive onside area run for a good 2-count by hundred-thousands: (Count: 101, 101; 101, 102). Then release to form a wall about 5 yards downfield from the line of scrimmage and at the perimeter. Block the first odd jersey to show back downfield away from the line.

ONSIDE GUARD: Executes the same as the tackle, but he gets 5 yards downfield from the onside tackle.

CENTER: Same as T, but he should get 5 yards downfield from the onside G.

OFFSIDE GUARD: Takes an inside release and clears the linebacker area. He gets to the normal defensive end position to the side of the "around" as fast as possible. The guard must hustle to get there, but he can get there. He sets up with his shoulders parallel to the sideline, but facing the play.

If the defensive end or the outside linebacker has gained depth, the offside guard must also. He keeps as much depth as he has. If the defender can make the play by moving on a perpendicular to the line of scrimmage, the offside guard will not be able to block him.

Unless the defender "smelled" out the play early, he will have to begin movement to the sideline. Once he does, the offside guard pops through his downfield breast.

The key to this block is patience and position. The element of surprise will take care of the rest.

OFFSIDE TACKLE: Bumps through the defensive tackle, then releases to the wall 5 yards downfield of the center. He executes the same technique as the rest of the wall once he gets there.

## Receivers

QUICK END: His job is to prevent whoever is responsible for his side third from getting to the wall.

SLOT BACK: Releases inside and gets to a depth about 7 yards behind the line of scrimmage. This depth should be attained before he gets to the center's position. Then he moves parallel to the line. He receives the pitch from the QB and takes note of the defensive end or outside linebacker. If the defender has "smelled" out the play and is able to cut him off, the SB does *not* belly deep to get outside him. Even if unsuccessful at beating the defender, the SB has given the rest of the defensive front time to diagnose and react to the play. Instead, he cuts hard upfield inside the defender. If this is unsuccessful, he still has a decent chance of getting outside to the wall.

If the defender has not properly read and reacted to the play, the SB should just take off and get to that wall

STRONG END: His job is to run off the defender in his outside third. Once he reads the around, the StE stalks him.

### Backfield

QUARTERBACK: Fakes the lead and pitches the ball to the slot back. The toss should be "soft" and should "lead" the slot. Once the toss is made, the QB immediately checks how the onside and the offside thirds are being covered.

OFFSIDE BACK: Fakes boot and gets downfield.

ONSIDE BACK: Fakes boot and gets downfield.

## The Blocking Pattern

### Line

ONSIDE TACKLE: Onside area run, wall.

ONSIDE GUARD: Onside area run, wall.

CENTER: Onside area run, wall.

OFFSIDE GUARD: Circle to first perimeter defender.

OFFSIDE TACKLE: Bump DT. Downfield.

### Receivers

QUICK END: Offside third.

SLOT BACK: Around.

STRONG END: Onside third.

### Backfield

QUARTERBACK: Fakes lead, makes toss, checks outside third coverage.

OFFSIDE BACK: Fakes boot, downfield.

ONSIDE BACK: Fakes boot, downfield.

## Play Look

See Diagram 7-3. Remember that the SB will break upfield hard if he reads that the DE or the OLB has read the play and can stop it by moving perpendicular to the LOS.

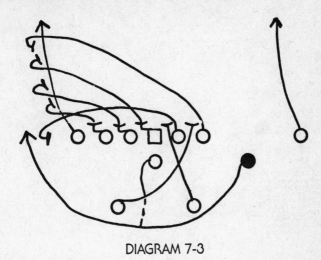

DIAGRAM 7-3

## Play Variations

The following are proven effective variations off the lead around.

### Lead around give

This is the same play as the lead, except instead of attacking the corner on boot action, the QB fakes a toss to the slot. The slot runs his around just as normal.

On the snap of the ball, both the offside guard and the tackle yell "reverse" as often and as loud as they can. This has a "hesitating" effect on the LB movement and offside pursuit, especially after the around is already run.

### Lead around pass

Here the around is faked and the quarterback drops, sets, and throws to one of the outside thirds. Usually the around is already run. Consequently, coverage in the outside thirds is seen and the QB knows which side he wishes to check first.

The line blocks exactly as they do in the boot pass. So do the set backs. The slot fakes around and continues to swing upfield. The ends fake their stalk, then attack deep. The lead back will be the safety valve. See Diagram 7-4.

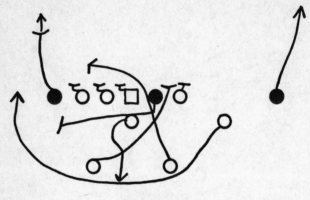

DIAGRAM 7-4

# 8

# Adapting the Perimeter Attack to the I

Using the same principles and concepts that are used in the lead and power series, the I formation can be utilized as an intricate part of the perimeter attack. An isolation attack can be run from the I, just as it is from split backs in the lead and power.

The objective is to force the defensive corner people (defensive ends, outside linebackers, cornerbacks, and defensive halfbacks) to commit or to overcommit to one of their run-pass responsibilities, and then to attack the other phase off a similar offensive action.

Personnel might be the reason to go to an I alignment, rather than a split look. The depth of the tailback in the I enhances his ability to read. It also provides a setting for the offense's best back to get his hands on the ball more often. What is lost is the effect of the quick pitch itself and the complementary series off it, but a perimeter game can still be run effectively.

## ISOTAK (ISOLATION-OFF-TACKLE)

### Play Objective

Here the off-tackle area is isolated. Veer principles are used in the blocking scheme, and the quick back (tailback) is given the opportunity to run for daylight. This is the base play in the series, and all other plays in the series will come off it. As the line blocks to the play and the slot or strong end seals inside, it presents problems to the defensive end or the outside linebacker.

## Position Responsibilities

### Line

The entire line blocks normal onside area run technique and assignment.

### Receivers

QUICK END:

*If onside or offside:* Blocks the outside third.

SLOT BACK:

*If onside:* Seals inside, blocking the first man to show. If that defender is being blocked by the quick tackle, he reads the quick tackle's head. If the quick tackle has outside leverage, the SB slides downfield to pick up the linebacker. He should expect him to be sliding behind the quick tackle's man or scraping off that defender's butt.

If the quick tackle does not have outside leverage on the defender, he must aggressively double-team that man.

*If offside:* Gets to the middle third.

STRONG END:

*If onside or offside:* Same as for the slot.

### Backfield

STRONG BACK (FULLBACK): Attacks the inside breast of the defensive end or the LB at top speed. If that defender slides inside with the seal block of the slot or strong end, he automatically attacks the outside breast and tries to hook the hips around to the outside.

## Note

He does not change his initial line to the defender. His point of aim is the defender's inside breast. If he seals inside, the strong back will be on the defender's inside breast or shoulder. The worst thing the back can do here is to hesitate.

QUICK BACK (TAILBACK): Begins movement parallel to the line of scrimmage. He will open step, crossover, and plant. His point of aim from that plant step is the outside hip of the tackle's block. As he begins movement to that outside hip, his eyes should focus inside the tackle until after the handoff is made. If daylight is read inside, he explodes to the inside hard. If it is not, his eyes now read the strong back's block. If he is kicking the defensive end or outside linebacker out, he breaks upfield inside the strong back's block perpendicular to the line of scrimmage. If the strong back is hooking the defender, he breaks upfield directly outside his block.

QUARTERBACK: Open steps on a 45-degree angle. He takes as large a step as possible and follows up with two more large steps to get good depth. The mesh points should be made as the quick back finishes his first step toward the line of scrimmage. The QB makes the handoff and attacks the perimeter, reading the play of the defensive secondary people who play the perimeter.

## The Blocking Pattern

*Line*

ENTIRE LINE: Onside area run.

*Receivers*

QUICK END:

> *If onside or offside:* Outside third.

SLOT BACK:

> *If onside:* Zone seal inside.
> *If offside:* Middle third.

*Backfield*

STRONG BACK (FULLBACK): Point of aim is inside breast of DE or OLE on alignment. Kick or hook.

## Base Play Look

In Diagram 8-1, the Isotak is run to the slot side versus a gap-4. This is a 173. For timing purposes, of course, the slot should take a minimum split—1 yard. Since the DT would seem to have outside leverage on the QT, a double-team would take place. A "seal" may also be called by the C, and the QkB could possibly read daylight for an inside break. The StB will either hook or kick out the outside LB, depending on how that player reacts to the play.

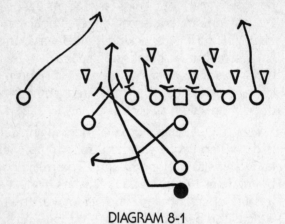

DIAGRAM 8-1

In Diagram 8-2, the StE will move to the LB, as long as he reads the strong T keeping outside leverage on the DT. If the StB hooks the DE, the QkB could break outside.

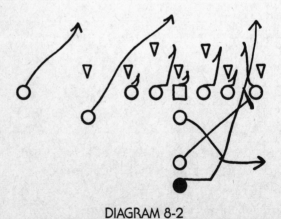

DIAGRAM 8-2

## ISOTAK CHARGE (ISOLATION-OFF-TACKLE KEEPER)

### Play Objective

In order to stop the Isotak, the defense must find a way to seal off both the off-tackle and off-end (slot) seams. The respect that the defensive people must pay to the off-tackle; plus the perimeter blocking scheme on the corner by the receivers; plus the long ride fake by the quarterback; plus the depth and proximity to the corner of the quarterback; will place tremendous pressure on the defensive perimeter. Motion can also add a nice wrinkle here.

### Position Responsibilities

#### Line

The entire line blocks the same as they do in the Isotak; onside area run.

#### Receivers

QUICK END:

> *If onside:* Blocks as he would normally in the pitch.

> *If offside:* Blocks the outside third.

SLOT BACK:

> *If onside:* Blocks the same as he would in the pitch.

> *If offside:* Blocks the middle third.

> *If in motion to onside:* Goes in motion on the QB's command. The ball will be snapped as the SB gets to the onside tackle's area. The SB attacks the outside breast of the first man to show outside the strong end's block.

> *If in motion to offside:* Turns upfield as soon as possible and tries to get to the middle third.

STRONG END:

> *If onside:* Same as normal pitch blocking. If aligned wide or medium, he seals inside. If aligned tight, he reaches the first man to show from head up to outside.

> *If offside:* Gets to the middle third.

*Backfield*

STRONG BACK (FULLBACK): The point of aim now is the outside breast of the defensive end or outside linebacker's alignment. However, as the StB nears that defender, he moves parallel to the line of scrimmage to get outside the block of the widest receiver. He attacks the outside breast of the first man to show. If he is going to the same side as the slot in motion, the StB checks his block on his defender. He must remember that the slot is attacking the outside breast of the same defender. If he has trouble, the StB should double-team him. If he is making the block, he seals inside checking pursuit. As in the Isotak, he does not slow up. He attacks the perimeter at top speed.

QUICK BACK (TAILBACK): Takes normal steps as in the Isotak. After the ride handoff fake, he continues on a line to the outside hip of the tackle. He keeps the outside shoulder dipped to hide the ball "pocket," but does not slow up. He hits the seam at top speed. He does not bend inside now, even if there is daylight there. If he is doing his job he should attract a crowd. This very much enhances the attack of the quarterback on the corner.

QUARTERBACK: Executes normal technique as he would in the Isotak. After a good ride fake, he pulls the ball off the front hip and begins the attack on the corner. He reads the block of the strong back and/or the slot on the corner.

## The Blocking Pattern

*Line*

ENTIRE LINE: Onside area run.

*Receivers*

QUICK END:

> *If onside:* Pitch.
> *If offside:* Outside third.

SLOT BACK:

> *If onside:* Pitch.
> *If offside:* Middle third.

*If in motion to onside:* Hits the outside breast of the first man to show outside the strong end's block.

STRONG END:

*If onside:* Pitch.

*If offside:* Middle third.

*Backfield*

STRONG BACK: Point of aim is outside the breast of the DE or the OLB. He breaks outside the receiver's block to the outside breast of the perimeter.

QUICK BACK: Fakes Isotak off-tackle.

QUARTERBACK: Fakes Isotak, attacks perimeter.

## Play Looks

In Diagram 8-3, the corner blocking is determined by that particular game plan's version of the pitch. In Diagram 8-4, the StE

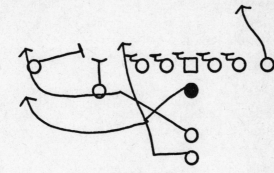

DIAGRAM 8-3

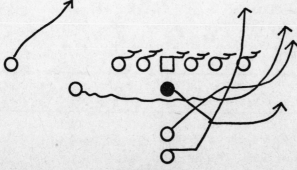

DIAGRAM 8-4

will reach if aligned tight as shown here, or will crack if split. The StB will not bypass anyone on the corner with whom the SB is having trouble. Diagram 8-3 shows a 173 charge, while Diagram 8-4 shows a 174 charge mo.

## ISOTAK PASS (ISOLATION-OFF-TACKLE PASS)

### Play Objective

As is true in the rest of our perimeter attack, the real pressure on the corner comes from the threat of a run-pass option. The Isotak pass gives us this off Isotak charge backfield action. This is really a pass first option. Motion can also be very effective.

### Position Responsibilities

#### Line

The entire line executes normal onside area pass concepts.

The wheel principle holds here for the center, the offside guard, and the tackle. The onside guard and the tackle should not wheel, in order to better simulate a run.

#### Receivers

QUICK END:

*If onside:* Gets a good release. Gets downfield and curls inside, finding the open area. Gets to a depth of about 15 yards.

*If offside:* Runs a post route through the middle third.

SLOT BACK:

*If onside:* Seals inside as if blocking for the Isotak or Isotak charge, then releases downfield and bends to the flat at a depth of about 8 yards.

*If offside:* Runs a crossing route. He tries to get to a depth of about 15 yards by the time he gets to the inside linebacker's normal curl zone. Once he gets that far, he throttles down in the open area.

*If in motion to onside:* Executes normal motion procedure and goes in motion on the quarterback's movement.

The ball will be snapped as he gets outside the strong end. He releases downfield and runs a curl at 15 and gets to the open area.

*If in motion to offside:* The ball should again be snapped as he passes the strong end. He runs a post through the middle third.

STRONG END:

*If onside or offside:* Executes the same release and route as the slot back.

## Backfield

STRONG BACK: Takes normal point of aim as in the Isotak charge. He runs directly at the outside breast of the defensive end or outside linebacker and works hard to get outside leverage and maintain the block. He does not slow up his attack.

## Note

The tremendous pressure put on the defensive end or the outside linebacker is critical here. In the Isotak, Isotak charge, and Isotak pass (and also in the Isotak sprint), the defender sees the exact same initial release of the strong end or the slot. He sees the exact same backfield action. He also sees the strong back attacking him in the same manner until he is about 2 yards away. In the Isotak, the defender is either being kicked out or hooked. In the Isotak charge, he is probably getting cracked upon from the outside and being bypassed by the strong back. In the Isotak pass, he is getting hooked by the strong back. In the Isotak sprint, he is getting cracked on from the outside and bypassed by the strong back.

With all this, keep in mind that the ballcarrier is either faking or running the ball directly to the defender's inside seam. The pressure is unbelievable when the play series is run properly.

QUICK BACK: Executes as in normal Isotak charge. However, if he clears the line of scrimmage, which he should not if the ride fake and his own "explosion" is well executed, he throttles down in the first open area to the outside. He does not go deeper than 5 yards.

QUARTERBACK: Executes steps and a good ride fake as in the Isotak charge. As soon as the ball is pulled, he continues the attack on the corner, reading the perimeter coverage. Both receivers should easily be in his line of vision. If they are covered, the QB runs the ball. He keeps in mind that this is a sprint principle. He does not slow up and is prepared to throw the ball on the run. He is conscious of proper sprint-passing fundamentals.

## The Blocking Pattern

### Line

ENTIRE LINE: Onside area pass.

### Receivers

QUICK END:

*If onside:* Curls at 15.

*If offside:* Posts.

SLOT BACK:

*If onside:* Seals inside, bends to 8.

*If offside:* Crosses at 15.

*If in motion to onside:* Curls at 15.

*If in motion to offside:* Posts.

STRONG END:

*If onside:* Seals inside, bends to 8.

*If offside:* Crosses to 15.

### Backfield

STRONG BACK: Attacks onside breast of DE or OLB.

QUICK BACK: Fakes Isotak charge. If possible, he gets to the dump area at 5.

QUARTERBACK: Fakes Isotak charge and reads the perimeter coverage. Passes first, runs second.

## Play Variation: Isotak Pass Throwback

This is the same as in many of the other play action schemes. Offside receivers can be predetermined as primary by the huddle call. Because of the sprint nature of the play, predetermining the backside receiver will force the quarterback to pull up after he begins a 2-3 step attack on the corner.

On the Isotak pass throwback, the quarterback reads the middle third coverage for the post first. If it's there, he throws. If it's not, he looks to the cross. Since this is called from the sidelines or the press box after the normal Isotak pass has been run a couple of times, the backside coverage has already been read. It would not be called if the coaching staff didn't feel that either one of the backside receivers would be wide open.

## Play Look

In Diagram 8-5, a 274 pass is set up. Remember that on a wheel technique by the backside G and T, they will either pivot back or drop perpendicular to the LOS, depending on the defense in their zones. If there is a defender in the passing lane on the curl, the QE will slide inside to the open spot.

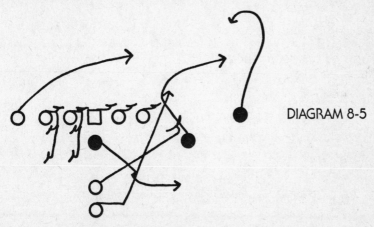

DIAGRAM 8-5

## ISOTAK SPRINT (ISOLATION-OFF-TACKLE SPRINT)

## Play Objective

This play is really a direct combination of the Isotak charge and the Isotak pass. Backfield action is identical to the rest of the series. The difference here is that a run-pass option is set up, but the receivers give run impression on their action. This is done to confuse the read of the secondary as they try to interpret their own run-pass keys. This is a run-first option off a sprint principle. A throwback call still exists as in the Isotak pass.

This play is devastating in goal line and short yardage situations. We find it most effective run to the quick side because of the seal of the quick end, or to the strong side with motion.

## Position Responsibilities

### Line

The line has the same jobs that they do in the Isotak pass. They execute an onside area pass concept with the center, playside guard, and tackle, not wheeling.

### Receivers

QUICK END:

*If onside:* Blocks pitch blocking as in the Isotak charge.

*If offside:* Posts to middle third.

SLOT BACK:

*If onside:* Executes as he does on the Isotak pass. He releases inside to simulate Isotak and Isotak charge, then bends to the flat at about 8.

*If offside:* He crosses to onside hook area to 15 yards. Throttles down in the open area.

*If in motion to onside:* The ball should be snapped as he gets just outside the strong end. As the ball is snapped, he will crack back on the defensive end or the outside linebacker. He keeps outside leverage on the defender.

*If in motion to offside:* Runs a post to the middle third.

STRONG END:

*If onside:* Releases inside and bends to the flat at 8, just as he would on the Isotak pass.

*If offside:* Crosses to the onside hook area. Gets to a depth of 15. Throttles down in the open area.

*Backfield*

STRONG BACK: Executes exactly as in the Isotak charge. This point of aim is the outside breast of the DE or the OLB. He bypasses that defender and attacks the outside breast of the first man to show outside the receiver's crack.

QUICK BACK: Executes as in the Isotak pass. However, he does not stop in the dump area. Instead, he continues as the QB continues no deeper than 5 yards. If he gets to the hash, he throttles down in the open area.

QUARTERBACK: Executes as in the Isotak charge, but looks to the bend or the quick back if contained.

## The Blocking Pattern

*Line*

ENTIRE LINE: Onside area pass.

*Receivers*

QUICK END:

> *If onside:* Pitch.
>
> *If offside:* Post.

SLOT BACK:

> *If onside:* Seals inside, bends to 8.
>
> *If offside:* Crosses to 15.
>
> *If in motion to onside:* Cracks to DE or OLB.
>
> *If in motion to offside:* Posts.

STRONG END:

> *If onside:* Releases inside, bends to 8.
>
> *If offside:* Crosses to 15.

*Backfield*

STRONG BACK: Isotak charge.

QUICK BACK: Isotak pass through dump to flat at 5.

QUARTERBACK: Isotak charge, but throws to bend or quick back if contained.

## Play Looks

Diagram 8-6 illustrates a 274 sprint, while Diagram 8-7 shows a 273 sprint mo. This play and the combination of these just mentioned—Isotak, Isotak charge, and Isotak—have been proven to be devastating on the corner. To really appreciate this, think of these as the defensive coach, who has to stop them, must.

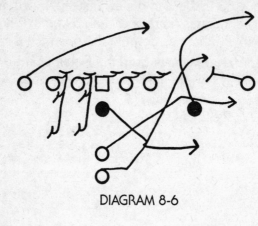

DIAGRAM 8-6

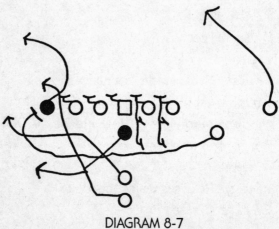

DIAGRAM 8-7

## ICE (ISOLATION)

## Play Objective

This play also initially comes off Isotak action. Counteraction by the quick back, and a reverse pivot by the quarterback, give the appearance of the Isotak. Besides being a part of the game series, it gives the offense the opportunity to take advantage of a quality back, who can read the opening.

The key here is for the quick back to read the defensive reaction to the blocking pattern, find an opening or "soft" spot in their reaction, and run for daylight. The point of attack is designed as the area between the offensive tackles.

## Position Responsibilities

### Line

ONSIDE TACKLE: First blocks anyone to his inside gap, as long as the defender is on the line of scrimmage. If there is no threat here, he takes anybody on his head or to his outside, then the LB.

ONSIDE GUARD: Has the same responsibility as the onside tackle.

CENTER: Blocks anyone to his backside gap as long as he is on the line. If there is no threat there, he blocks on first, and then works his way to the frontside gap. If no one is there, he blocks the LB.

OFFSIDE GUARD: Blocks on first, then to his outside, then LB.

OFFSIDE TACKLE: Has the same responsibility as the offside guard.

## Note 1

The entire line should be aggressively attacking the breast to the side of the natural angle, which will be the near breast. Against a man who is head up, seek outside leverage, but do not be concerned if leverage is gotten inside depending on the defender's technique and responsibility. If that is the case, take the man in the direction he wished to go.

## Note 2

For purposes of position responsibilities and blocking patterns, we designate an "onside" and "offside" by play direction given in the huddle. Keep in mind, however, that the point of attack is anywhere between the offensive tackles. This depends on the runner's judgment.

*Receivers*

QUICK END:

*If onside or offside:* Blocks the outside third.

SLOT BACK:

*If onside or offside:* Blocks the middle third.

STRONG END:

*If onside or offside:* Blocks the outside third.

*Backfield*

STRONG BACK: Aggressively attacks the first vacant seam to the onside. If both the center-guard and the guard-tackle seams are occupied, he attacks the inside breast of the first man to show outside the tackle's block.

QUICK BACK: He must be sure his alignment is not too loose to the strong back. There is a tendency here for the quick back to do this, especially if he doesn't usually run from an I alignment. Too close an alignment to the strong back may impede the runner's ability to read daylight.

He countersteps parallel to the line. He pushes off that "counter" foot, and bangs back to the line of scrimmage. He reads his key.

Versus an odd defense, he keys the nose guard. Versus an even set, he keys the defensive guard. Versus a double-gap scheme around that guard, he reads the backside defensive guard. If his offensive guard is also double-gapped, he breaks upfield hard directly inside the block of the strong back.

QUARTERBACK: He reverses his pivot and gets as much depth as he possibly can. The pivot should take him just to the offside of the center's hip. He makes the handoff and fakes his attack to the corner.

## The Blocking Pattern

*Line*

ONSIDE TACKLE: Inside gap on the LOS, on, outside, LB.

ONSIDE GUARD: Inside gap on the LOS, on, outside, LB.

CENTER: Backside gap on the LOS, on, frontside gap, LB.

OFFSIDE GUARD: On, outside, LB.

OFFSIDE TACKLE: On, outside, LB.

### Receivers

QUICK END:

> *If onside or offside:* Outside third.

SLOT BACK:

> *If onside or offside:* Outside third.

STRONG END:

> *If onside or offside:* Outside third.

### Backfield

STRONG BACK: Takes first vacant seam to onside, first defender outside the tackle.

QUICK BACK: Countersteps, reads key, and goes to daylight.

QUARTERBACK: Reverses handoff, attacks perimeter.

## Play Look

See Diagrams 8-8, 8-9, and 8-10 for an Ice to the strong side (176). In 8-8, the onside G could possibly double the NG or the DT depending on the defensive recognition calls made by the C or the

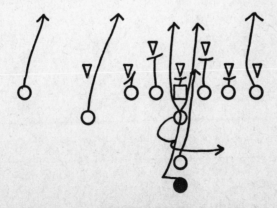

DIAGRAM 8-8

T. The offside G could double the backside DT depending on the offside T's call. The QkB will read the NG as his key.

In 8-9, the blocking is very obvious against that gap-4 look.

In 8-10, the onside T could double the DT if the outside G gives an "out" call. The C will block the backside LB.

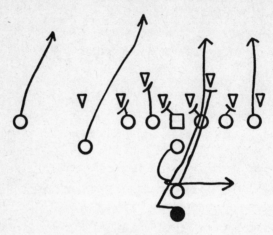

DIAGRAM 8-9

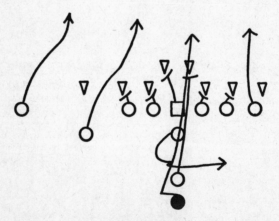

DIAGRAM 8-10

## ICE DIVE

### Play Objective

This is a quick-hitting counterplay to the strong back that comes off Isotak action. The nature of the series tends to force lateral movement by the linebackers. This quick hitting inside forces them not to leave too early. As with the Ice, there is no specific point of attack. The strong back runs for daylight between the offensive guards.

## Position Responsibilities

### Line

ONSIDE TACKLE: Executes a slide technique. Drives off the line at the linebacker, preventing penetration of any near defender to his inside. He leads with his inside foot. He will not be blocking anyone who is aligned in his inside gap. By the same token, he is not blocking anyone head up, unless that defender tries to get the onside tackle inside. Then he must work hard to keep inside leverage. He attacks the near breast of the near linebacker.

ONSIDE GUARD: Blocks the inside gap aggressively first. If there is no threat there, he blocks anyone head up. If there is not threat there, he slides to a linebacker. He uses a similar technique as the onside tackle. If he *and* the offside guard have double-gap calls, he crosses with the center.

CENTER: Blocks on as a first priority. If there is nobody to block, he aggressively blocks the playside gap on the line. If no one is there, he blocks the offside gap on the line. If no one is there, he blocks the near linebacker.

If both guards give double-gap calls, he crosses with the onside guard.

OFFSIDE GUARD: Blocks similarly to the onside guard. However, if both the offside guard and the onside guard give double-gap calls, the offside guard reaches the playside gap. He uses a normal onside area run technique here.

OFFSIDE TACKLE: He has the same responsibility and technique as the onside tackle.

### Receivers

All receivers have the exact same jobs as they do in the Ice.

*Backfield*

STRONG BACK: Takes a quick counterstep parallel to the line. He pushes hard off that "counter" foot and attacks the area between the guards. He reads his key.

Versus an odd set, his key is the nose guard. Versus any other gap or even defense, he hits the first vacant seam between the tackles. He hits the onside seams as a priority if both are open. Versus "quadruple gaps" around both guards, the center and the onside guard will cross. He attacks through the guard's butt on alignment.

QUICK BACK: Fakes the Isotak to the offside. This will be the same direction that the quarterback will begin his pivot.

QUARTERBACK: Takes a quick, short, reverse pivot. Hands off to the strong back and attacks the perimeter. On that reverse pivot, he must be sure to have pivoted wide enough so as to clear the strong back's path and allow him to read daylight.

## The Blocking Pattern

*Line*

ONSIDE TACKLE: Slides.

ONSIDE GUARD: Gap, on, slides, crosses with center versus "quadruple gaps."

CENTER: On, up gap on the LOS, back gap on the LOS near LB, crosses with onside guard versus "quadruple gaps."

OFFSIDE GUARD: Gap, on, slides. Onside area run (reach) versus "quadruple gaps."

OFFSIDE TACKLE: Slides.

*Receivers*

Same as the Ice.

*Backfield*

STRONG BACK: Countersteps, reads key and goes to daylight.

QUICK BACK: Fakes Isotak offside.

QUARTERBACK: Reverses pivot, hands off, attacks the perimeter.

## Play Look

See Diagrams 8-11, 8-12, 8-13, and 8-14 for the Ice dive to the strong side (178). The *slide* technique is demonstrated by the guards and tackles in Diagram 8-11, the tackles in Diagram 8-12, the guards and tackles in Diagram 8-13, and the tackles again in Diagram 8-14. This technique has proven to be a great weapon on the two quickest inside hitting plays in the offense—the *sneak* and

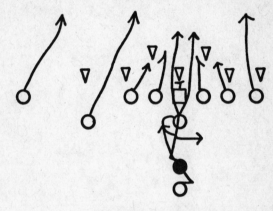

DIAGRAM 8-11

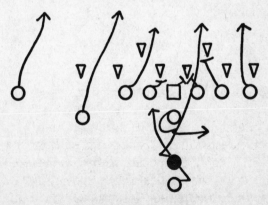

DIAGRAM 8-12

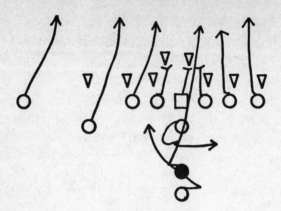

DIAGRAM 8-13

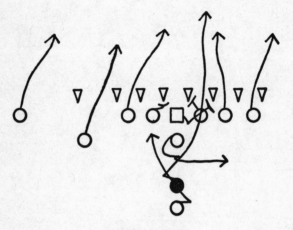

DIAGRAM 8-14

the *Ice dive.* As long as the defensive lineman doesn't cross the face of the offensive blocker to the inside, the runner will clear the defender. Generally, splits will be maximum here.

The hairiest situation on paper here is in Diagram 8-13, where no defensive lineman is blocked. If the guards execute the *slide* properly, the defensive tackles will *not* get to the StB. The other advantage is the obvious one: If the runner clears the LB area, he has a lot of help downfield for a break away.

## ICE LEAD

This play is almost identical to the normal lead from the split backs. The line and receivers have exactly the same position responsibilities and blocking pattern as they do in the lead. The only change is in the backfield's timing, which is necessary because of the change of alignment.

The strong back has the same job as the onside or lead back in the lead. The quick back has the same job as the running back. He should predetermine the point of attack, open step, and use the inside hip of the strong back as his pivot of aim.

The quarterback must vary his pivot so as to (1) gain greater depth, and (2) get more to 180 degrees.

Since the point of attack is now predetermined, just as in the lead, but not as in the Ice, it might behoove the quick back to tighten his alignment closer to the line of scrimmage. The Ice lead may prove more effective than the Ice when you don't have a back who can read daylight, or when you don't want the back to read daylight.

Refer back to Chapter Five for greater detail on the lead.

# 9

# Optioning the Perimeter

Most teams in modern-day football attack defensive perimeters in one form or another through their option games. The purpose here, however, is not to reiterate information already found in the books written on the triple option, the veer option, the belly option, the speed option, or the counter option. Instead, the following option series is one that is specifically part of the perimeter attack package. Many of the principles upon which it is based come directly off the pitch and the perimeter schemes already described and analyzed.

Motion can also prove advantageous here in terms of the strongside option attack.

The following plays will be analyzed:

> Option
> Option Pass
> Ride Option
> I-Options

## OPTION

**Play Objective**

In our actual scheme the *option* is really part of the *pitch* series. Like the pitch, it can be run with the backs set in a quick, strong, or split alignment. Whatever alignment we are running the pitch from will also determine what the option will be run from. Remember, the play is not designed to be run to the quick side from a weak alignment, or to the strong side from a quick alignment, unless setback motion is utilized.

The option is geared to look initially exactly like the pitch. As noted in Chapter Two, the only way defenses will stop the pitch is by the quality of inside-out pursuit and immediate, tight, aggressive containment. The option attacks the man responsible for that containment by optioning him. It is also designed to cut off that inside-outside pursuit.

Thinking back to the pitch series, keep in mind once again the tremendous pressure placed on the perimeter defender. Not only does the pitch cause him an immediate problem, the pitch pass, pitch read, pitch trailer, ride pass, and ride charge take advantage of what he must do if he is to successfully stop the pitch. That same perimeter defender is now being optioned, instead of the normal defensive end.

### Position Responsibilities
### (When run to the quick side from either
### a quick or split backfield set)

*Line*

The entire line blocks exactly as they do on the pitch switch. The onside tackle does not pull, but blocks the onside area run, as do the quick guard, center, and strong guard. The offside or strong tackle gets downfield to the track or middle third.

*Receivers*

QUICK END: Blocks the same as in normal pitch blocking. However, if at all possible, we prefer a "switch" call. This gives the advantage of both a seal and "runoff" block on the corner.

SLOT BACK: Blocks the same as in normal pitch blocking. We prefer a "switch" call, if possible. On the switch, the SB arc releases as he would on the pitch. He runs at the outside breast of the contain man, but bypasses him to get downfield to the auxiliary contain man. The defender responsible for the auxiliary contain will either be coming from the outside third, or the middle third on an inside-out concept.

In an effort to keep his leverage, this should have a widening effect on the perimeter defender. This creates a seam to the inside. The SB should keep in mind also that the perimeter defender will be reacting to the lead back. This is the back that normally gets the ball on the pitch. He is not the pitch back on the option, however.

If the perimeter defender super cheats or comes on a predetermined stunt and beats the slot out, the slot should immediately turn upfield and play the first defender to show from inside out. He looks for a linebacker on his scrape or pursuit, or a safety working on an invert principle.

STRONG END: Like in the pitch, the StE simulates a screen, or attacks the backside third.

## Backfield

LEAD BACK (QUICK BACK): He must remember that this is normally the pitch back in the pitch. He releases parallel to the line the same as he does in the pitch. He should be looking back to the quarterback to simulate the pitch.

He begins with an open step, crossover, and plant. On that third step he breaks hard to the line right outside the block of the quick end. He clears his block and looks inside for the near linebacker immediately. He seals him from the track. He will be there. If he is not there yet, he moves toward him to make the seal and keeps outside leverage.

If there is no "switch" call, he expects the linebacker to get picked up by either the slot or the quick end. If that is the case, he checks to make sure the linebacker has been blocked. If he hasn't, he seals him. If the linebacker has, he continues to auxiliary containment.

PITCH BACK (STRONG BACK): He cannot pace the play. He stays parallel to the line of scrimmage and goes as hard and as fast as possible. He keeps that "5-yard pitch relationship" to the quarterback, as if tied to a stick. He expects the pitch to be made often times, after he has crossed the line. He expects a bad pitch.

QUARTERBACK: The QB does not shuffle as he does in the pitch. He does, however, show a "body lean" as he does in the pitch. He comes out to about a depth of about 3 yards. This should occur on the QB's third step.

He begins to open, crossover, and plant. He immediately focuses attention on containment. He does not slow up; there will be a strong tendency to do so. He attacks outside the quick end's block. As he turns upfield, he works outside on a 45-degree angle. This will keep him moving away from the inside pursuit that would hit him blind side. He considers a cutback only after the linebacker area is cleared.

He should pitch the ball early only if containment obviously plays him. The QB will pitch the ball downfield on instinct, but he always keeps the following principles in mind: (1) he already has gained yardage, so he will pitch only if he feels he has the big gainer; (2) he *never* risks a bad pitch; (3) he looks before he makes the pitch; (4) if he breaks into the secondary, he is probably 1 on 1 with a defender. The QB can beat him by himself—he shouldn't become "pitch happy."

## The Blocking Pattern (To the Quick Side)

### Line

ENTIRE LINE: Blocks pitch switch (even if the "switch" is not called by the receivers).

### Receivers

QUICK END: Blocks pitch. Thinks pitch switch.

SLOT BACK: Blocks pitch. Thinks pitch switch. On the pitch switch, he bypasses primary containment to auxiliary containment.

STRONG END: pitch.

### Backfield

LEAD BACK (QUICK BACK): Fakes pitch release and seals the near linebacker downfield off the quick end's block. If there is no LB, he attacks the auxiliary containment.

PITCH BACK: (STRONG BACK): He will pitch back.

QUARTERBACK: He will "body lean" the pitch. He comes out on
a 45. He attacks outside the quick end. Option containment. He goes back to a 45 after clearing the line.

### Play Look (To the Quick Side)

See Diagram 9-1 for an option quick (161). The line blocks
normal onside area run, and the StE either attacks the middle third
or sets for the screen as he does in the pitch. The SB bypasses
primary containment to auxiliary containment that could come
from outside or inside, depending on the secondary's run support.
The primary contain men will be optioned, and the QB must *not*
slow up as there is a tendency to do.

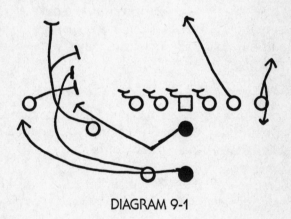

DIAGRAM 9-1

### The Option to the Strong Side
### (Must be run from a strong or split backfield set)

#### Line

The entire line really has the same job. There is one exception,
however. The strong tackle may switch responsibilities with the
strong end. The strong end will seal inside to the linebacker. If he
can't get there, he will block down on the strong tackle's man. The
strong tackle will then loop around the strong end and get to a
linebacker seal position, or attack the linebacker directly if he can
get him and take away outside leverage.

### Receivers

The quick end and the slot block do exactly the same as they do in the pitch when they are offside. The strong end seals inside to the linebacker. If he can't get there, he blocks inside to the first man to show. The tackle then takes the linebacker, either directly or by a loop seal.

### Backfield

The lead back (strong back) attacks the outside breast of the first perimeter defender to show outside the defensive end. His initial steps should simulate the pitch.

The pitch back (quick back) does the exact same thing as the strong back does when the strong back is the pitch back. This time, however, he expects to get the ball much sooner than when the pitch back does when the option is run to the quick side.

The quarterback has the same job, except he reads the defensive end now. His point of aim is the inside shoulder of the defensive end.

### Play Look

When operating from a strong and quick backfield set, it is most effective to shift to the strong set from the quick. If operating from the split, it doesn't really matter if he comes out in a split or shifts to it.

See Diagram 9-2 for 162. Exactly how the StE and the ST block their area depends on how they read that area of the defense. Since the QB and the StB have to travel less of a distance to get to the perimeter, it is a faster-paced option than the quickside attack.

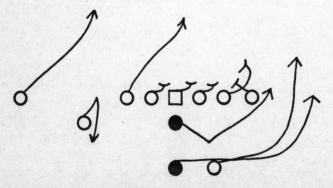

DIAGRAM 9-2

## The Option to the Strong Side with Motion
## (Must be run from a strong or split backfield set)

Depending on personnel or game plan, the slot, when in motion, can: (1) Seal the linebacker. If this is the case, no other responsibilities would change. (2) Attack the first man to show on the perimeter outside the defensive end. If this happens, the lead back will: (A) finish off that defender; (B) seal the LB; (C) attack the outside breast of the defensive end. If he hooks the DE, the quarterback options the first man to show outside that block. (3) Crack back to seal off the defensive end. If that happens, the quarterback options the first man outside him.

## OPTION PASS

### Play Objective

This is geared to specifically attack the defensive perimeter. Once the offensive coaching staff sees how the defense is playing the option and its variations, the same option will be simulated in a play action scheme.

If certain patterns best attack a particular defensive scheme, the routes will be called. To the quick side, the first route always refers to the slot or quick end, depending on who is running the pattern. The second route is for the quick back. To the strong side, motion will always be used, and the motion route is given first. The strong end's route is second. This allows the flexibility to determine the most advantageous patterns in a game.

For example, when running option pass to the quick side, *option pass post-out* refers to the slot running a post and the quick back the out. When running it to the strong side, option pass post-out tells the slot in motion to run the post, and the strong end to run the out.

However, the following have proven most effective in the past, and are a predetermined part of the option pass package:

Flood
Hook—Out
X
Backside Route

## Position Responsibilities
## (When play is being run to the quick side)

### Note

For timing purposes, the best backfield alignment would be quick. If split or strong is used, backfield motion should be used.

### Line

The entire line blocks the onside area pass. The frontside should not wheel.

### Receivers

QUICK END AND SLOT BACK: One receiver blocks; the other releases to run a pattern. Whoever runs the pattern initially steps as he would on the option, before his actual release. What determines who blocks and who runs the pattern is how the option is run in that particular game. A *switch* call is preferred.

STRONG END: Runs either a deep or cross at his own discretion. If he sees he will definitely be open, he immediately brings this to the attention of the quarterback or the coach.

### Backfield

LEAD BACK (QUICK BACK): Runs exactly as he does in the option initially. Once he gets to the linebacker seal position, he runs the pattern.

STRONG BACK: Begins as he would in the option. He then attacks the first odd jersey to show outside the quick tackle. He attacks his outside breast, moves at top speed, and does not slow up on contact.

QUARTERBACK: He attacks the corner as he would in the option. On his third step he continues to gain depth in behind the strong back. He reads the normal "to-be-optioned" defender. If he is up, he thinks pass. If he plays off, he thinks run. He executes the play with proper sprint technique.

## The Blocking Pattern (to the Quick Side)

*Line*

ENTIRE LINE: Onside area pass.

*Receivers*

QUICK END: Blocks option or runs pattern. Thinks switch.

SLOT BACK: Blocks option or runs patterns. Thinks switch.

*Backfield*

LEAD BACK (QUICK BACK): Fakes option. Runs pattern.

STRONG BACK: Fakes option. He is the first defender to show
outside the quick tackle.

QUARTERBACK: Fakes option and makes the pass-run attack
on perimeter.

## Pattern Variations and Looks
## (To the Quick Side)

*Option pass flood*

See Diagram 9-3. The slot (or quick end) runs an out at 10.
The quick back runs an intermediate flag. He begins the flag at 10.
Diagram 9-3 shows a normal switch release by the slot.

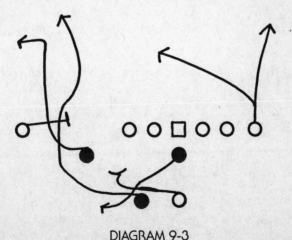

DIAGRAM 9-3

### Option pass hook-out

See Diagram 9-4. The quick end (or slot) hooks in at 17. The quick back runs an out at 8. There is no "switch" call here.

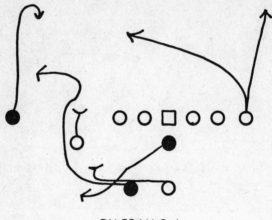

DIAGRAM 9-4

### Option pass X

See Diagram 9-5. The slot (or quick end) posts at 8. The quick back runs the intermediate flag at 8. Here a "switch" call does take place.

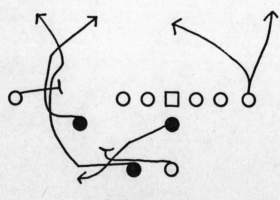

DIAGRAM 9-5

### Backside routes

If the strong end sees he will be open, the backside pattern will be called. Once it is called, it becomes the primary pattern. On a *deep,* he attacks the backside seam. If he sees the middle third open, he posts. On a *cross,* he gets to the onside curl area at a depth of about 15. He will throttle down in the open area. For example, option pass flood deep means option pass flood will be run to the quick side, but the quarterback will pull up early and try to hit the strong end on a deep. If the deep is not open, the QB will check off to the frontside patterns.

### Red call

This is a designation for the backside strong end to stay in and block. His rule is onside area pass wheel. This will obviously be used to give the quarterback extra backfield protection.

## The Option Pass to the Strong Side

Here motion will be used. Backfield alignment can be either strong or split. A shift from the quick would be most effective here.

### Line

The entire line is still onside area pass. The frontside should not wheel.

### Receivers

Patterns will always be called. The slot's pattern is called first. The strong end runs his route off an inside release. He will be simulating his option seal of the linebacker.

The backside quick end does the same thing as the strong end when the strong end is offside.

### Backfield

LEAD BACK (STRONG BACK): Begins arc release to simulate option. Then he aggressively attacks the outside breast of the first man to show outside the strong tackle's block.

QUICK BACK: Moves parallel to the line of scrimmage at top speed. He reads the block of the strong back. If the strong back has successfully gained outside leverage, he continues to flare as a safety valve. If the strong back hasn't, the QB finishes off the defender.

QUARTERBACK: Executes just as he would to the quick side. He has a pass-run option on the defensive perimeter.

*Play look: option pass strong jet-bend*

See Diagram 9-6 for a 162 pass-jet-bend mo. Keep in mind that a shift here from quick to strong back would be effective.

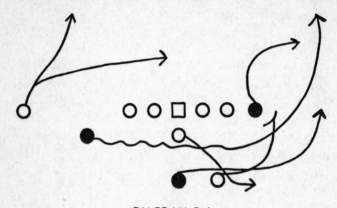

DIAGRAM 9-6

## RIDE OPTION

### Play Objective

The purpose of the ride option is to option attack the weak side of the backfield alignment. It attacks the strong side from a quick alignment and the quick side from a strong. From a split it attacks either side and can be treated similarly to an outside veer theory.

Steps and timing from a quick or strong are similar to that of a ride in the pitch series.

Motion can be effective, but would not be used to the offside.

### Position Responsibilities

*Line*

ONSIDE TACKLE: Blocks the first man to the inside. He does not block *on.* If he is supposed to block a linebacker, but can't be there, he looks around his outside neighbor and uses a seal technique.

ONSIDE GUARD: Same as onside tackle.

CENTER: Same as onside tackle.

OFFSIDE GUARD: Pulls inside and attacks the outside breast of the first man to show in containment outside of the defensive end. The defensive end is not being blocked. He must be sure not to hesitate. He moves at top speed and does not slow up in that defensive end area.

OFFSIDE TACKLE: Blocks onside area run.

## Receivers

QUICK END:

*If onside:* Attacks the outside third.

*If offside:* Blocks the outside third.

SLOT BACK:

*If onside:* Blocks the first man to his inside.

*If offside:* Blocks the middle third.

*If in motion to onside:* Blocks the outside breast of the first man to show outside the defensive end.

STRONG END:

*If onside:* Blocks the first man to his inside.

*If offside:* Blocks the outside third.

## Backfield

ONSIDE BACK: This is the ride back. He will open, crossover, and plant. He attacks the area immediately to the outside hip of the slot (or strong end). He keeps the outside shoulder dipped and hits the seam at top speed. He expects to be hit by the defensive end.

OFFSIDE BACK: He is the pitch back. He stays parallel to the line, keeping the proper pitch relationship with the quarterback. He runs as hard and as fast as possible.

QUARTERBACK: Opens with depth and steps as he would in the actual ride. He gives a good ride fake. He attacks the corner. He tries to get outside the defensive end or his own. He should be reacting inside to the ride back.

If he clears the defensive end, he executes the same fundamentals as he would in the option to the quick side.

## The Blocking Pattern

### Line

ONSIDE TACKLE: First man inside. He loops to a seal if he can't get to a LB.

ONSIDE GUARD: First man inside. Loops to a seal if he can't get to a LB.

CENTER: First man backside. Loops to a seal if he can't get to a LB.

OFFSIDE GUARD: Pulls and attacks the first man outside the DE.

OFFSIDE TACKLE: Onside area run.

### Receivers

QUICK END:

*If onside or offside:* Outside third.

SLOT BACK:

*If onside:* First man inside.

*If offside:* Middle third.

*If in motion to onside:* Attacks first defender to show outside DE.

STRONG END:

*If onside:* First man inside.

*If offside:* Outside third.

### Backfield

ONSIDE BACK: Rides outside strong end or slot's block.

OFFSIDE BACK: Pitch back in option.

QUARTERBACK: Fakes ride. Option perimeter.

## Play Look

See Diagram 9-7. Note how both the onside tackle and the center may have difficulty getting to the Oklahoma linebackers.

They *loop to a seal* technique. This may look, at first glance, as though the "loop" technique allows an alley for the linebackers to blitz. Keep in mind that blitzing linebackers have proven most ineffective against the base perimeter game of this offense. Consequently, very little blitzing is used. If the T or C in Diagram 9-7 anticipates a blitz, they would *not* loop. Their loop technique does *not* have to be communicated to anyone else.

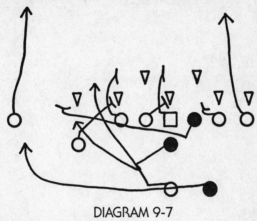

DIAGRAM 9-7

## Ride Option Give

As long as the frontside executes, the only defender that can readily play the ride back with any consistent success is the defensive end. The ride option is predicated upon him reacting to the ride. If he does not, the *ride option give* is executed exactly like the ride option except the quarterback gives the ball to the onside back. The QB then fakes the option on the corner. There is no change for anyone else.

## ADAPTING THE OPTION TO THE I

As mentioned in the beginning of this chapter, normal option schemes will not be analyzed here. For those coaches who run an I and wish to take advantage of some of the concepts discussed in Chapter Eight, the option schemes discussed in this chapter can be adapted.

The option, option pass, and ride option are all as adaptable to an I club as are the more conventional belly and dive option theories.

# 10

# Destroying the Defense with an Option Air Attack

Most of the passing in this book is dedicated to attacking the defensive perimeter. A complete offense must also be able to attack other areas of the defense by air as well. Whenever the book diverts from attacking the defensive perimeter, it does so to take advantage of defenders who have dual responsibility, as is the case in the lead and the power series. Not to take advantage of such defenders is not quality offensive football. This chapter attempts to *option* defenders through the air and over the entire range of the field.

Offensive football, in its most sophisticated form, is an ability to attack a defensive scheme *after* the ball is snapped. It is only then, after the ball goes live, that the defense must begin its actual execution.

Assuming there isn't a tremendous mismatch in personnel, no defense can completely take away both the run and pass. No pass defense can be so designed so as to adequately cover short, intermediate, and deep routes, while at the same time key the screen and the draw and still put good pressure on the quarterback. To be able to read a particular defensive weakness after the ball has been snapped provides a tremendous advantage.

Many good dropback passing games attempt to accomplish a similar objective. After the ball has been snapped, the quarterback and the receivers must determine and analyze the coverage. To develop such an air attack adequately is a most difficult task, however. To begin with, it is a tough job for both the QB and the receiver to correctly read pass coverages in an instant. This is precisely the reason why it takes so long to develop an adequate pro QB. It takes experience to get the feel for reading and reacting to specific defenses in pressure situations. It is also difficult to perfect the timing between passer and receiver due to the large number of patterns that must be mastered.

An air attack would be effective if it could be condensed to do as follows:

1. Attack all areas of the field. This would take better advantage of field position and prevent the defense from cheating or overcompensating to a particular man or zone.

2. Limit the number of patterns in an effort to increase the proficiency and attack principle of the pattern. This would also aid the timing of the quarterback and the receiver.

3. Isolate any attack area by giving specific keys that could be read without great difficulty.

4. Incorporate the draw and the screen into the attack scheme in order to take advantage of dropping linebackers and "all-out" pass rushes.

5. Execute the four above concepts off *one* base call (except for a separate screen designation).

Would this then not prove to be a most effective air attack? It could be mastered in practice and executed in games *after* the snap of the ball. This is the type of passing game that will be developed in this chapter.

The defense will tell us what routes will be run. The defense will tell us who the primary and the secondary receivers are. The defense will tell us how many receivers will run routes. The critical point here is that all this will be done by optioning the defense after the snap of the ball.

## AIR OPTION

### Play Objective

In a normal dropback scheme, it makes sense to throw the "quick pop" when a linebacker fills. It also makes sense to run a draw when the linebacker drops. This is the premise upon with the *air option* is predicted.

There are just so many things a defense can do. By isolating the LB first, a specific read key is given to the QB. As the LB reacts to the play, the QB executes his key, taking advantage of what the LB gives up.

The QB is involved in a logical, three-step progression key. That key is based on an *inside-out read theory* and the isolation of a specific defender or area. Each receiver has an attack principle that is an intricate part of each pattern. These patterns, when coordinated with the QB read, allow the offense to take advantage of the entire playing field, thus spreading out the defense.

The fact that no receiver has more than three patterns to run, and the QB has no more than four patterns to throw, gives an opportunity to develop the proper timing on these in practice.

Since the greatest pass defense is pressure on the passer, a top priority here must be adequate protection for the quarterback. At no time will the rush be in a situation where defenders will outnumber blockers, without giving the QB ample time to release the football. This assumes, of course, that the defense doesn't rush nine or more men.

## Play Call

In the huddle, after the formation has been determined, the play call will be given as "air option strong" or "air option quick." The strong or quick will designate the attack side of the defense. That side can really be considered the onside. The offside is the side opposite the attack side.

## Line Protection Responsibilities and Techniques

### Responsibilities

CENTER: Blocks the nose. If none, he blocks the defensive guard in either of his gaps. If both gaps are occupied, he blocks the offside gap. If the gaps aren't occupied, he picks up a LB who fires through his seam. If no linebackers come, he should never stand around. He attacks the first pass rusher to penetrate inside. If no one does so, he attacks the closest pass rusher to him from the inside out, or he goes downfield on the QB's "go."

GUARDS: Blocks the DG. If aligned in double-gaps, they block to the offside. If there are no defensive guards, they pick up a LB who fires through their area. If no LB fires, they attack the first pass rusher to come into their area. If no one comes, they attack the center's man. If the center's man is handled, they attack the tackle's man or go downfield on the QB's "go."

TACKLES: They block the defensive tackle. If aligned in double gaps, they block to the offside. They should never double-team the inside gap, if it means leaving the outside gap unprotected. If there are no defensive tackles, they pick up a LB who fires through their area. If no LB fires, they attack the first pass rusher to come into their area. If no one comes, they attack the guard's man, or go downfield on the QB's "go."

## Defensive line definitions for the air option

NOSE GUARD (NG): Any defensive man on the line aligned over the head, eye, or ear of the center, but not on his shoulder.

DEFENSIVE GUARD (DG): Any defensive man on the LOS from the outside shoulder of the C to the inside shoulder of the T.

DEFENSIVE TACKLE (DT): Any defensive man on the LOS from the outside shoulder of the G to the inside shoulder of the strong end or the slot. Note the area between the G and the T where a defensive lineman can be considered both a DG and DT.

LINEBACKER (LB): The defensive man who aligns behind the defensive line in a position that is most definitely off the LOS. The LB will always be in a two-point stance, but the MG, DG, or DT can be in an up or down stance.

*Blocking pattern for the
offensive line on air option*

CENTER: NG; DG; offside versus gaps; LB; inside penetration on "go."

GUARDS: DG; offside versus gaps; LB; area penetration on "go."

TACKLES: DT; offside versus gaps (but never double-team inside if outside gap is threatened); LB; area penetration on "go."

*Pass blocking technique for the line*

All pass blocking on the LOS is man-to-man. Therefore, it will always be very simple to see whose man put pressure on the QB.

If his opponent is head up or outside, the lineman takes one short drop-step with his outside foot. If his opponent is inside, he takes that same step with his inside foot. If the C's man favors one side, he drop-steps to that side. If he is head up, he does not drop-step until he forces one side or the other.

He sets quickly with a low center of gravity, live feet, head up, fists by nipples, and elbows out. He must always be under control and keep balanced.

The lineman does not attack the defender, but forces him to commit himself first. He keeps live feet and a low center of gravity, and seeks contact without lunging. As the lineman's "toes step on his toes," he "bites his near nipple." He continues to "bite that nipple," while working for leverage where his body is between the defender and the quarterback.

Once pressure from the defender is felt, he drives the defender in the direction that his own body momentum has taken. He does not attempt to drive unless that pressure has been felt. Should the defender change the direction of his rush before pressure is felt, he seeks leverage to the near side. Then he repeats the just-noted procedure.

Once he begins his drive, he never allows the defender to cut back across his face. He does not hold, but uses his arms as wings to "lock" on the defender. As he drives, he keeps that good base, that center of gravity, and live feet.

He may employ a cut block, but only as a change up against a very hard-charging defender who likes to go through the line. In that case, the lineman cuts just prior to "biting the nipple"—as "his toes reach the lineman's toes." When he cuts, he pops right up. He never stays on the ground.

## Note

Keep in mind that this is *not* the usual hit-recoil-hit principle of most dropback pass blocking techniques. It is, however, the most appropriate for the *air option*. This will become clearer as the chapter's concepts develop.

### Technique coaching points for the line

POSITION: Initial steps.

CONTACT: As "his toes reach the lineman's toes," and he prepares to "bite the nipple."

PRESSURE: As he "bites the nipple," and pressure is felt against his face.

LEVERAGE: As pressure is felt and he "locks up" with the defender.

DRIVE: Once leverage and pressure are achieved, he takes the man in the direction of his body momentum.

### Fundamental coaching points for the line

LOW CENTER OF GRAVITY: Butt is kept low.

WIDE BASE: Feet are kept at shoulder width or a little wider.

LIVE FEET: Short, choppy, piston-like steps must be taken at all times.

BALANCE: Shoulders and arms should stay relatively parallel to the ground.

HEAD UP: Neck should be bulled with eyes up.

## Setback Protection

The best backfield alignment is split in regards to simplicity of execution. However, either strong or quick can be almost as functional.

### Responsibilities and techniques

Responsibilities here are the same for both the strong back and the quick back.

As the ball is snapped, the strong or quick steps with his inside foot and reads the linebacker to his side. If the linebacker fires, he attacks him immediately from the inside out. He wants leverage through his inside breast.

If the linebacker does not come, or if he is picked up by a lineman, he pushes off the inside foot. He moves outside parallel to the line of scrimmage and attacks the inside breast of the first man to show outside the tackle's block. He comes under control just prior to contact. Contact and leverage must be maintained on this defender in a similar fashion as the line blocking technique.

As the line may, he may cut the defender as a change of pace. He must be prepared to get up immediately.

If there is no one to block, he *flares*. This will be described later in detail.

### Blocking pattern for the set backs

BACKS: Inside—LB; outside—E/OLB, flare.

## Protection Looks Versus Various Defensive Fronts

See Diagrams 10-1 through 10-4. *Assume in each that the quick side is the attack side and that the quick side is to the right.*

In Diagram 10-1 versus a straight Oklahoma fifty, the center has the nose. The guards take the linebackers if they fire or scrape; if they don't come, they play area penetration. The tackles take the defensive tackles. The backs should realize that, except for an unusual LB stunt, they will not have to pick up the linebackers. The guards will do that. The backs will play the defensive ends if they come. If they don't, they flare.

DIAGRAM 10-1

In Diagram 10-2 versus a gap-6, the center has a double-gap call. He blocks the defensive guard to the offside. The offensive guards block the defensive guards, which means the strong guard and the center double-team the defensive guard. The tackles have the defensive tackles. The backs check for linebacker fire. If there is none, they move to pick up the defensive end. If they don't come, they flare.

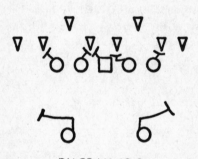

DIAGRAM 10-2

In Diagram 10-3, a split-4 is attacked. The center will pick up the linebacker if he comes. If both come, he reacts offside. The guards take the defensive guard. The tackles technically may have double-gaps, but they never double the inside gap, if it will leave the outside gap uncovered. They block their outside gap. The strong left back will not have to worry about the linebacker coming, since the center would pick him up. He goes directly to the outside linebacker (who is treated exactly like a defensive end). If that end does not come, he will flare. The quick right back checks LB, then end, then flares.

DIAGRAM 10-3

In Diagram 10-4, against a 60-gap stack, there is no nose, so the center takes the defensive guard. The strong (left) guard has the double-gap so he blocks away from the call. The quick (right) guard takes the defensive guard. The strong (left) tackle has the double-gap also, so he blocks away from the call. The quick (right) tackle must block outside versus double-gaps since he can't block inside and leave the outside uncovered. The strong (left) back will flare and the quick (right) back plays linebacker, then defensive end, or flares.

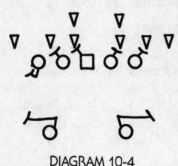

DIAGRAM 10-4

## Receiver Responsibilities and Techniques

### Pattern attack principles

STRONG END:

*If onside:* Gets release while keying the inside LB to his side. If he fires, he runs the pop and attacks the short middle. If he does anything else, he runs a comeback from 12 to 10. He attacks the short to intermediate outside.

*If offside:* Gets release and drives to the deep middle. He checks personal coverage.

SLOT BACK:

*If onside:* Gets release while keying the inside LB to his side. If he fires, he runs the pop. If he does anything else, he runs the jet, attacking the deep outside.

*If offside:* Releases and drives to the deep middle. He checks personal coverage.

QUICK END:

*If onside:* Releases and does comeback from 12 to 10 from the LOS, or from 14 to 12 from his alignment.

*If offside:* Releases and jets. Checks personal coverage.

QUICK BACK: Whether onside or offside, if there is no blocking responsibility, he will run flare. He turns upfield immediately outside the tackle's block. However, if the T takes the defender deep into the backfield, he turns upfield inside the T and checks personal coverage.

STRONG BACK: Same as for the quick back.

*Pattern attack technique*

THE POP: The receiver attacks the short middle by taking advantage of the area vacated by the inside LB. He bends inside but never goes further inside than the offensive tackle to his side. This might allow a defender from the offside to defend the pop. He continues on a line vertical with the OT. See Diagram 10-5.

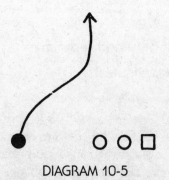

DIAGRAM 10-5

THE COMEBACK: The receiver runs it hard downfield at a perpendicular to the line of scrimmage, if possible. If there is a defender in the area that the pattern is being run to, he runs at his outside breast. At 12 yards, he comes under control and comes back hard on a 45-degree angle to the outside pushing off the inside foot. He looks for the ball immediately *on* the break, *not after the break has been made.* The ball should be released *on* the break. See Diagram 10-6, point A to B.

If the ball has not been released by third step, he pushes off the inside foot and turns back upfield. He may very well be open in this intermediate zone. See Diagram 10-6, point B to C.

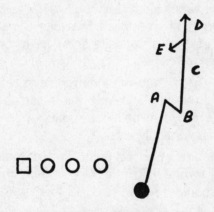

DIAGRAM 10-6

As he runs deep, he stays to the outside. If at 20 yards, he can beat his defender deep, he continues. He he can't, he breaks back, pushing off the outside foot with hands up on a collision angle with the quarterback and the line of scrimmage. See Diagram 10-6, point C to D or E.

If the quarterback starts to run and gets past the LOS, the receiver becomes a blocker. If he does not pass the line, he moves on an angle with him.

THE DRIVE: This is a pattern that attacks and isolates the deep and intermediate middle third. It can be run by the strong end or the slot. Basically, the deep third can be covered with a three-deep zone, two-deep zone, or man-to-man.

After the release, he takes a direct angle to the middle third of the field at a depth of about 15 yards. He reads the coverage of that deep third as soon as possible.

If the secondary plays too deep, he splits the deep defenders by running to the middle of the offensive alignment in a vertical line with the center. Then he breaks hard upfield. This new angle should be to an area between the defenders covering the deep halves.

If the secondary plays three deep, he runs directly at the middle safety. He runs again at a point about 15 yards downfield in a vertical line with the center, then breaks upfield toward that safety. He does not allow himself to go to a head-up position with him. Instead, he seeks leverage to one side or the other. He seeks opposite shoulder to opposite shoulder leverage.

If playing man-to-man, he runs at that point once again in front of the center. This will bring the defender on him to the middle of the field. As he breaks upfield, he treats the defender the same as a middle safety.

While running to that point 15 yards in front of the center, he checks for the ball. If the QB can't get the ball to the pop man, he should be open from 12 to 15 yards.

Regardless of the coverage, he should break back after 20 yards. If he doesn't have the defenders, he should beat deep. See Diagram 10-7.

DIAGRAM 10-7

THE JET: This is a pattern run by any of three quick receivers. It attacks and isolates the deep and intermediate outside half.

If the secondary is playing zone in that area, he must first determine whether or not the deep defender can play him near the sideline. If he can, the receiver runs at his outside breast, attaining outside-in vertical leverage. This will leave an open area between the receiver and the sideline. See Diagram 10-8. If the defender is already hugging the sideline, the receiver attacks his inside breast and works for inside-out horizontal leverage. See Diagram 10-9.

If the defender would find it difficult to cover the receiver, he stretches the seam and hugs the sideline. This forces the DB to go a long way to get to the ball. See Diagram 10-10.

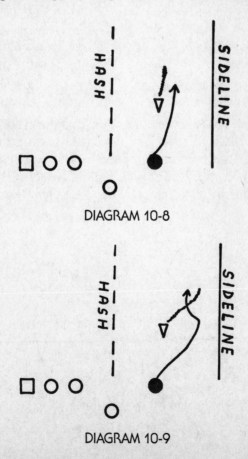

DIAGRAM 10-8

DIAGRAM 10-9

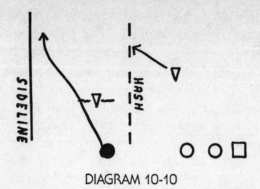

DIAGRAM 10-10

If he is being played man-to-man, the receiver treats the defender as if he could cover him in a deep zone. He seeks inside or outside shoulder to shoulder leverage. If taking leverage inside the defender, he must be sure he is close to the sideline or force him there.

Regardless of coverage, if the ball has not been released by 20 yards, he breaks back if he can't beat the defender deep.

FLARE: This tries to take advantage of the short and intermediate zones, and is run by the set backs.

As the back turns upfield, he keys the inside LB. If the LB is in a position to cover him, he attacks his outside breast, then breaks to the inside looking over the inside shoulder for the ball. He does not break inside more than where the normal OT would be on alignment. (Note the quick back in Diagram 10-11.)

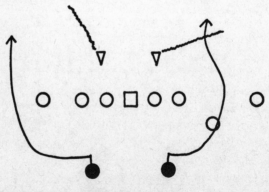

DIAGRAM 10-11

If the LB cannot cover him, he widens the seam and forces him to come a long distance. (Note the strong back in Diagram 10-11.)

## A Most Important Coaching Note

On all patterns, there is an effort to try to get a specific side leverage on the defender. The QB will always throw the ball at the side to which the receiver has leverage. This enables the receiver always to have himself between the ball and any defender.

### Release technique

An excellent way to defend a pop pass is to not allow the receiver a release off the LOS. Preventing a receiver's release can also hamper the QB-receiver timing. The proper release off the LOS is critical as part of our attack. This is the first part of the pattern attack principle.

If no one is preventing the receiver's release, he simply explodes off the LOS. If one man is, but he feels he can release outside him, he makes a typical arc release to the outside: open, crossover, and plant. He makes the movement parallel to the line. By that third step, he explodes off the line at top speed.

If the receiver's judgment dictates an outside release would be better, he open steps to the inside and explodes. As he does so, he "makes himself skinny." Normally his shoulders would be parallel to the ground. He turns them in such a way as to make them perpendicular to the ground. His back should be turned to the outside.

### Break-back technique

If the QB is going to throw deep, he will have done so by the time the receiver has taken the pattern 20 yards. By that time, he should know whether or not he can beat his defender deep. If he can, he continues the pattern. If he can't, he comes under control and points back toward the QB, pushing off the away side foot.

As he breaks back, he gets his hands up and moves in the direction of the QB and the LOS. He continues this route until the QB passes the LOS, then he becomes a blocker.

If the QB leaves his "pocket" to move outside, he changes the direction of his break-back angle. See Diagram 10-12.

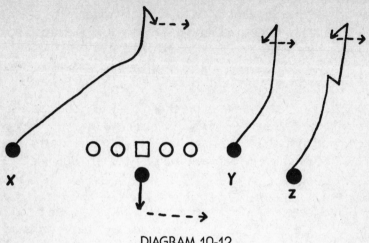

DIAGRAM 10-12

*Further receiving techniques*

These are just a few emphasis points on fundamentals.

INTENSE CONCENTRATION: This is probably the most important single factor a receiver must have to be a great one. From the moment the ball leaves the QB's hand, or as soon as the ball is picked up after the break, he focuses complete attention on the tapered end of the ball.

When the QB is holding the ball, he doesn't just look at the QB; he looks at the ball. The eyes and head should look the ball into the hands, while the mind focuses every fibre within the body to think of the tapered end of the ball.

BREAK CONCENTRATION: Too many receivers look for the ball after the break in their pattern is made—it's too late then. *As* the break is made, he makes it sharply with hands up in a catching position. Head, hands, body, and mind think ball *as* the break is made sharply.

CROSS FINGERS: It is very important to keep the hands together in receiving the ball. When faking the QB, thumbs should be crossed on all balls thrown below the waist or over the shoulder.

BODY: While the body aids in catching the football, it does not catch it—the hands do. Use the body to "trap" a ball only when absolutely necessary. The receiver should "concentrate" the ball to the hands and then quickly cradle it to the body.

Since the hands do the catching, the receiver does not allow a defender to do anything that will allow him to interfere with his hands and arms. He always keeps his body between the defender and the ball.

## QUARTERBACK RESPONSIBILITIES AND TECHNIQUES

### QB Attack Principles and Reads

In order to give the impression that the QB is reading the entire defense, he begins his drop by backpedaling as quickly as he can.

As he gets under the center, he checks the inside linebackers to both sides. Just before he signals for the ball, he focuses attention on his first key.

His first key is the onside-inside LB. If the LB fires, he thinks *pop*. The inside-out read principle of the QB is a simple one. He has a good line of vision from the ball to the receiver, or to where the receiver is going. That line of vision is the *ball flight line*. His immediate concentration is on that ball flight line. If it is occupied, or if the threat of occupying that line exists, he immediately checks off to drive.

If the pop is covered from the outside-in, he still goes to the pop but throws the ball inside the receiver, who is on a track vertical to the alignment of the offensive tackle. If he isn't covered, he gets the ball to him as quickly as possible.

When looking for the drive, he exercises the same read. If open early, he reads the ball flight line. If covered, he gets the ball deep. Whenever throwing the ball deep, he arcs the ball with a high release as deep and as high down the field as possible. When throwing to the middle third, he throws the ball to the side that the receiver is on—the shoulder over which the receiver is looking. He will normally have a 5 to 10-yard cushion or margin for error or all deep passes.

If the LB does anything else but fire, the QB will immediately focus complete attention to the comeback and read the ball flight line. If uncovered, he will release the ball as the receiver comes under control, to the point at which he will finish his pattern. If covered, he looks inside immediately from tackle to tackle. Since the LB did not fire, there will be a running lane someplace—the QB must find it. He explodes through that running lane on a QB draw.

While running toward the LOS, he may still throw the ball to the comeback and up, the drive, the jet, and the flare. By this time, the drive and the jet will have started their break back. He releases the ball quickly while moving toward the LOS, but stops and comes under control to go deep. Of course, he must always know where the LOS is.

## Coaching Note

If your quarterback either doesn't have respectable running ability, or you just don't want to risk him by running him on the QB draw principle, simply develop a checkoff passing priority for him to follow in regard to the other patterns. The exact order of priority here depends on the specific offense and the passing game that you run.

For our purposes here, we will assume that the QB will be used as a runner when his keys tell him to exercise his QB draw principle.

## Summation: QB Attack Principles and Reads

Before the snap, key the LB:

If the LB comes, pop.

If the pop is covered, drive.

If the LB does not come, key comeback.

If covered, key running lane (or check off to secondary receivers).

As the QB draw begins, he will check off to any pattern at his discretion.

## QB Dropback Technique

The QB begins to drop as quickly as possible from a backpedal position. Once the LB is read, the QB looks for the pattern. On the pop, he stops, pivots and sets as soon as he picks up the pop receiver. This should be at 3 to 5 yards.

If the LB doesn't come, he continues to drop, keying the comeback; he will stop, pivot, and set right before the receiver begins to come under control. This should be at 5 to 7 yards.

All normal passing fundamentals apply here. He must be sure to "target" and "frame" the receiver.

### The Arc Pass Drill

To drill the middle third arc, the QB stands in the center of the field and throws the ball over the goal posts. He begins shallow, but gains depth as his confidence and arm develop.

To drill the outside third arc, he throws over the goal posts from the sidelines.

Once again, all proper passing techniques apply here.

Please note, however, that when throwing to a break-back or flare pattern, the QB must get the ball as quickly as possible to the receiver's chin. He never just throws at the receiver; he always targets and frames him.

### Play Variations

To change the air option principles would defeat many of the things we are trying to accomplish. However, each receiver is to check and know his personal coverage. If he finds that he is not being covered, his pattern could become the QB's second read. This way, we are always taking advantage of what the defense gives us, without changing our own play.

For example, on *air option drive,* all patterns are exactly the same as the air option. The QB takes his first key on the LB as always; if the LB doesn't come he reads the ball flight line of the drive; if uncovered, he gets the ball there immediately; if covered, he finds running land to draw with the same check-off option to throw.

### "Go" Call

In certain situations, it may prove an advantage not to allow the QB an option to throw once he begins his draw move. The "go" signal is a key to the offensive lineman to go downfield when uncovered, instead of blocking the inside penetration. This may be given as a call in the huddle or during the play.

## A Critical Coaching Note

Since this play never changes, it will become imperative for the coaching staff to be able to analyze how the defense is stopping the play it, or how they are adjusting to it, if the coach is to utilize maximum efficiency in attacking the defense. Communication between the sideline and the press box, during games and between players and coaches, is critical. Each receiver must know, understand, and be able to report what his personal coverage is. For example: The LB does not fire, but holds his position off the LOS. The comeback is covered, and the LB stops the QB on the draw. If he is on or near the LOS, he cannot cover the drive or the flare. We can either caution the QB to look for the flare as he begins his draw, or go to an air option drive call.

## "Red" Call

Whenever a hard four-man defensive rush comes from the offside, we should still be in good enough shape to handle it. However, whenever an extra pass protector is desired, "red" is attached to the call. This indicates that the offside strong end or slot stays in to block. He blocks the first man outside the OT's block. If the call would be *air option strong red,* the slot would go red.

## Grounding the Ball for the QB

We don't want our QB to take any unnecessary punishment, nor do we want him thrown for a loss, nor do we want him to throw the ball up for grabs.

If the QB is in trouble and cannot get to a running lane or pass to an open receiver, he should get rid of the ball as long as he still has movement of his throwing arm. When throwing the ball into the middle of the field, he should throw it in the general area of a receiver, but nowhere near any defenders. He should drill it low and hard. When throwing the ball toward the sidelines, he should get it out of bounds. Some extra "movement" behind the LOS is permissible here as long as yardage is not lost.

However, the QB *never* just blindly releases the ball into a crowd. He must always *know* what he is doing. Poise is one of the QB's most important assets; he must never lose it. Throwing the ball blindly often results in either an interception or a penalty, and an intentional grounding penalty is a severe one. He must be prepared to eat the ball in those situations where he must.

## Some Base Play Looks

In both Diagrams 10-13 and 10-14, assume that the call is air option quick. Diagram 10-13, the strong end drive, is an effort to force the middle third deep and to be a secondary receiver to the pop. If the QB pops to the slot, the strong end is in great position to block. If it is the middle third that tries to play the slot in the pop, the strong end should have a score on the QB check off from the pop.

Since the LB fires, the slot will pop. Remember that this cannot be bent too far inside. If the QB checks off from the pop, the slot will go deep. He will then break back at 20.

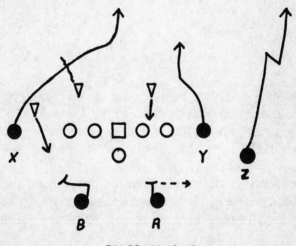

DIAGRAM 10-13

The quick end runs a comeback. Since the QB will not be reading the comeback, he will turn upfield off his third step. The quick back will pick up the LB, unless an uncovered lineman does so. If that is the case, the quick back checks outside to block or to flare. The strong back will pick up the defensive end since he is coming.

In Diagram 10-14, the strong end drives and the quick end runs his comeback. Since the attack side LB does not fire, the comeback is now the primary receiver. Also, since the LB does not come, the slot jets.

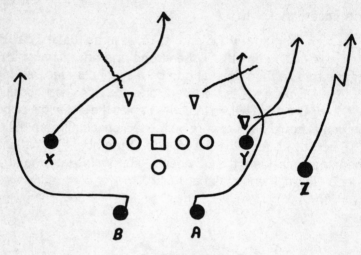

DIAGRAM 10-14

The quick back has no responsibility to either the LB or the defensive end, since both drop. Since the LB looks like he is wide enough to cover him, the flare will break to the inside after attacking that LB's outside. The quick back is now in a perfect spot to receive a pass or block for a QB draw.

The actual huddle calls here for both would be 292. The strong back will keep his flare wide, assuming he reads that the near LB's drop is not wide enough to play him adequately.

## AIR OPTION SCREEN

### Play Objective

With the immense pressure placed on the linebackers and the secondary in the air option, it normally will not prove effective for the defense to send the linebackers on an all-out blitz. They would be needed to play, or aid in playing, the pop, flare, and drive.

By the same token, it is not in the defense's best interest to give the QB too much time to throw. Consequently, the defense will need a quality rush from at least its front, to defend the air option screen that it is designed to take advantage of.

The screen can go to either the strong or quick back, and comes directly off the air option. All alignment points that held true for the air option would also be true for the air option screen.

## Position Responsibilities

### Line

The entire line blocks exactly as they do in the air option, except they employ the screen technique.

### Receivers

QUICK END:

*If onside or offside:* Jet.

SLOT BACK:

*If onside:* Keys the LB for the pop exactly as he would in the air option. If the LB does anything else, he runs a deep.

*If offside:* Drive.

STRONG END: Executes the same job as the slot back.

### Backfield

QUICK BACK:

*If onside:* Reads the LB as in the air option. If the LB comes, he attacks him, and the normal air option is on. If the LB does anything else, he pushes off the inside foot moving parallel to the line. If the defensive end or the outside linebacker is coming, he attacks his inside breast. He uses good screen technique as he is passed by after contact. "Slip" to the screen area. If there is no outside pressure, he begins to run wide flare, and then throttles down in the screen area.

*If offside:* Executes exactly the same as in the air option.

STRONG BACK: Exactly the same as the quick back.

QUARTERBACK: Reads attack side LB as he would on the air option. If the LB comes, he executes pop and drive reads as normal. If he does anything else, he continues to drop, so as to give the screen time to form. He looks "off" the onside initially and executes screen.

## The Blocking Pattern

### Line

ONSIDE TACKLE: Air option, screen release to containment.

ONSIDE GUARD: Air option, screen release to inside-out force.

CENTER: Air option, screen release to clean up "garbage."

OFFSIDE GUARD: Air option.

OFFSIDE TACKLE: Air option.

### Receivers

QUICK END:

If onside or offside: Jet.

SLOT BACK:

If onside: Key LB, pop, or deep.

If offside: Drive.

STRONG END: Same as slot back.

### Backfield

QUICK BACK:

If onside: Reads LB for block. Defensive end or flare to screen.

If offside: Air option.

STRONG BACK: Same as quick back.

QUARTERBACK: Read LB for pop or drive; screen.

## Play Look

See Diagram 10-15. Assume *air option screen strong.* Remember here that if the LB came, the QB, strong end, and strong back would all execute normal air option. The huddle call here is 293.

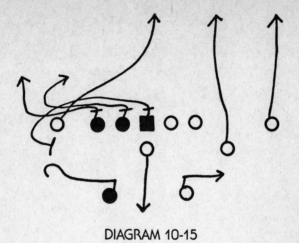

DIAGRAM 10-15

# 11

## Attacking the Defenses Loaded with Great People

There comes a time in the careers of most coaches when they are faced with the prospect of playing a team whose people are far superior to their own. What does a coach do when the defense is strong and quick enough to totally control the inside; when they are fast and tough enough to seal the corner from the outside-in and choke off any running lanes from the inside-out; and when the under, intermediate, and deep coverage tends to be all over the receivers, if indeed, the QB has time to get the ball off at all? The really bright coach is the one who makes sure his athletic director doesn't schedule such teams.

For those of us, however, who not always blessed with that type of cooperation, a difficult and demanding challenge presents itself. The feeling here is that no matter what happens, it is imperative to keep in mind that panic is the worst thing that can happen. It is a major error now to get away from basics. It is even more important to be sure that the basic execution of fundamentals is there; otherwise, offensive adaptions in terms of a game plan will prove ineffective, regardless of how well thought out or sound those adaptions might be.

In the beginning of this book, I said that while this entire offensive package is used on the field in one form or another, obviously the *entire* package is not part of the offense each and every season. Going into each season, the strengths and weaknesses of our personnel are evaluated in detail, as are the overall strengths and weaknesses of our opponents. Based on the results of these evaluations, the specific offensive package for that season is established. Then that package becomes very specifically refined for each game. It would be against everything the perimeter attack philosophy believes in to change that package just because we are facing a team that is without question better than we are.

By the same token, we have to admit that something has to be done, at the very least, to try to equalize the odds. Consequently, the series to be discussed in this chapter, known as the *special series,* is built directly into our overall offensive package and resulting game plan.

Our special series does *not* represent major changes for our players, although it appears to be very different. Every day in team offensive work, at practice, ten minutes is spent on the special series. That ten minutes has proven adequate time to execute the series effectively.

As much as we hate to admit it, there are those times where our offense completely bogs down. In the perimeter attack scheme, a system of play calling, which will be discussed in the next chapter, dictates whether our running game will attack inside or outside. As that game becomes established the play action passing game is used to complement that attack. If an apparent weakness is spotted in the defense or if the defense is so good personnel-wise to shut down a running game that puts tremendous pressure on specific defensive weaknesses, then the opponents are attacked through the option air game. If they are good enough to take that away, we are either in for a long day, or we better come up with something that they just can't defend. The special series is what we came up with, the breakdown of which follows.

## ALIGNMENT

At first, there were two different alignments used; specific plays came off each. The feeling was that two different looks for a series such as this defeated one of the most important requirements of the series; namely, quality execution of something that appeared to be totally different, but wasn't that difficult for our players to learn.

This gave us one formation, which was called to the left and right, which was important to us since it determined which side our quick and strong personnel went to. Even here, though, we felt that cutting the series down to one call without direction would simplify things even further and thereby enhance our execution and practice organization. The results are shown in Diagrams 11-1 and 11-2.

In the huddle, the term *"special"* designates the formation. "Special," however, is followed by the hash designation of the ball. The QB determines whether or not the ball is on the hash or in the middle of the field. The general rule of thumb he is given is that if the ball is within 3 yards of the hash, consider it on the hash. Therefore, if the QB determines the ball is on the left hash, the formation call in the huddle is "special-left hash"; if on the right, it is "special-right hash"; and if not on the hash, it is "special-middle."

When the ball is considered on the hash, the quick side always goes to the wide side, while the strong side goes into the boundary. When the ball is considered "middle," the quick side goes to the right, and the strong side to the left. The alignment of the quick side remains relatively standard, with the QT split 10 yards from the QG, and the QE and the SB split 2 yards from the QT. The strong side has a similar alignment on a "middle" hash call—the strong tackle aligns 10 yards from the StG with the StE 2 yards outside of him (Diagram 11-1). On "right" or "left" hash call, the StT aligns 1 yard from the StG with the StE 4 yards outside of him (Diagram 11-2).

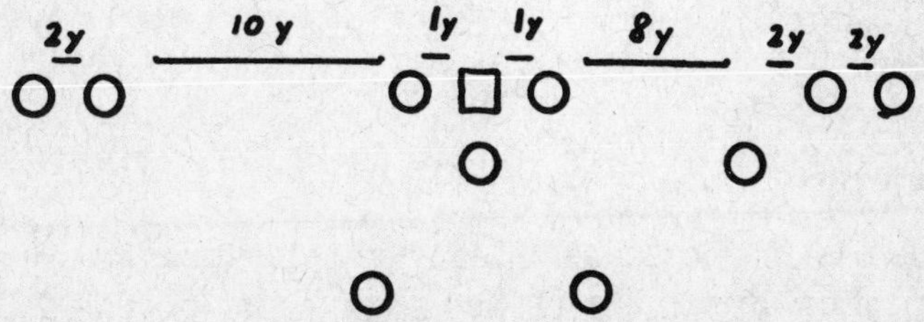

DIAGRAM 11-1

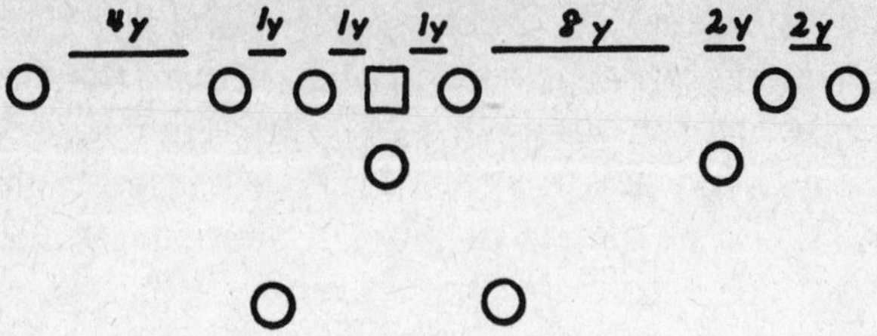

$$\overset{8y}{\text{O}} \overline{\phantom{xxxx}} \overset{1y}{\text{O}} \overset{1y}{\text{O}} \overset{1y}{\square} \text{O} \overline{\phantom{xx}} \overset{8y}{\phantom{x}} \overline{\phantom{xx}} \overset{2y}{\text{O}} \overset{2y}{\text{O}}$$

DIAGRAM 11-2

## FLY AND MOTION

As with the regular offense, fly and motion can be put into effect here. Mo designates normal motion by the SB across the formation on the QB's "look." Fly designates normal motion by one of the set backs across the formation also on the QB's "look." Which set back goes *fly* will be preunderstood and determined by the actual play call.

## PLAYS ADAPTED TO THE SPECIAL SERIES

The following are the base plays that can be executed easily and effectively in the special series:

Sneak
Lead
Pitch
Pitch Pass
Pass
Screen

## SNEAK

### Play Objective

There is an immediate tendency by most defensive teams to align most of their men in the same areas occupied by the alignment of the offensive formation. The ball itself is really the area that has to be defended first and given top priority. In Chapter One, the *sneak* is broken down and analyzed. At that time it was pointed out to what extent the sneak is emphasized as a very important part of the offense. We practice it every day and run it effectively in games. If the team is not adequately playing the middle of the formation, there is no better, simpler way to attack that area than the sneak. Of course, both mo and fly can also be used here.

## Position Responsibilities and Blocking Patterns

This is really the same as outlined in Chapter One. Both guards block gap, on, slide, while the center blocks on, up gap on LOS, back gap on the LOS near LB. Versus quadruple gaps, the C and the onside G cross.

The people aligned outside the guards work hard to get to the middle third on a 45-degree angle, trying not to allow a potential tackler to cross their face and keeping their mind on the possibility that the QB may cut across field behind their blocks after he gains decent positive yardage. The set backs will work downfield outside the guards' blocks. They should not block anybody they come in contact with on the LOS. The QB will make the same read and hit the same hole that he would in a normal sneak call.

## Base Play Look

Every team will play the special differently. Rather than diagram each play against a multitude of looks, we will look at just the base look for each play in this series. See Diagram 11-3 for a sneak right. Remember the QB has a variety of seams he can attack, depending on the looks the defense gives him.

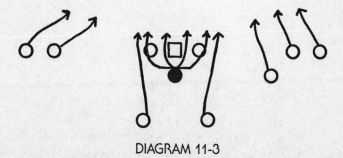

DIAGRAM 11-3

## LEAD

### Play Objective

Obviously, this can be run only to the strong side and only if the ball is called on a hash. The lead is a quality, safe play to run in a series that seems quite unorthodox. While fly can't be used here, motion can be.

### Position Responsibilities and Blocking Patterns

For the StT through the QG, the QB, and the set backs, there is no change here from the normal lead blocking pattern explained earlier. The outside people attack the middle third using a similar technique to what they would use in the sneak.

### Base Play Look

See Diagram 11-4 for "special-left hash," lead left."

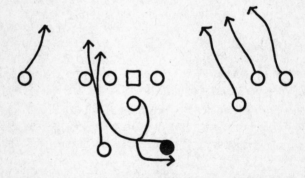

DIAGRAM 11-4

### Coach's Note

As stated at the beginning of this chapter, the perimeter attack turns to the special series when faced with problems. Since the offense is very successful, the series does not have to be run too often. However, if the series were to be further developed, one of the first plays I would want to add would be the *boot off the lead.* It would always be run to the quick side when the ball is on the hash. It would be run very similar to how the boot is normally done. The SB, QT, and QE would block similarly to how they would in the special series pitch, which will be explained next. While the boot has not been used as part of the series, it is interesting to think about the effectiveness of it if implemented.

## PITCH OR PITCH PASS

### Play Objective

When looking at the pitch from this series, it is imperative to keep two things in mind to understand the philosophy and overall soundness of the scheme. First of all, if the defense is giving the middle away, it will be taken advantage of via the sneak and the lead. Second, when the pitch was analyzed earlier, it was noted that there is an area from outside the block of the onside guard, who is executing an onside area run technique, to a point outside at the normal tackle's alignment, where the pitch can't be knocked down. In the special series, this means there is an area of about 4 yards outside the onside guard's alignment that technically does not have to be blocked except for the technique of the onside guard. The reasons for this are explained in detail in Chapter Two.

Consequently, when the pitch is run, it is run most effectively. I stress this point because it does not appear that way on paper. In reality, however, it is a potent weapon.

Whether or not the pitch or the pitch pass is run comes down to the type of personnel you have in your backfield. Ideally, the pitch pass is the play the offense would want to take advantage of because of the tremendous run-pass option pressure it puts on the perimeter of the defense. Fly has proven tremendously effective here, but mo can also be used.

### Position Responsibilities and Block Patterns
### for the Pitch

The center and both guards block onside area run as they do normally. If the strong tackle is wide, he has the same block as the quick tackle, assuming he is onside; namely, he attacks the near breast of the first defender to show on or off the LOS to his inside. If the StT is onside and tight, he pulls to attack the outside breast of the first man to show on the corner. If the SB is onside, he also blocks the near breast of the first defender to show on or off the LOS to his inside. The ends, if onside, will block the first defender to show outside the tackle's block. If there is a fly back, he serves as the pulling tackle would in a normal pitch situation. The QB executes as normal, as does the RB who cuts upfield hard at the first sign of daylight. It is most important that the RB attack the corner at top speed, and not look for daylight at a controlled speed.

### Position Responsibilities and Blocking Patterns for the Pitch Pass

The entire line from tackle to tackle blocks the same as they do in the pitch as just explained, except there is no movement off the LOS to go downfield. The SB also begins as he does in the pitch. If he comes into contact with a defender at the LOS, he holds the block; otherwise, he bends back outside to the intermediate flat at a depth of about 12 yards.

The onside end runs a jet, while the offside end posts. The offside back should generally go fly and will execute as he did in the pitch, where he attacks the first man to show on the corner. The QB makes the pitch and releases immediately to the flat where he tries to move parallel to the movement of the RB.

The RB thinks run, but as long as he hasn't committed to the run, the ball should be held up similar to how the QB would on a sprint. The RB should never think run while he reads the outside third. If a receiver is open, he should take advantage of it. The QB as a receiver should be used primarily as a safety valve. The backside end on a post would generally be taken advantage of only if a predetermined call is made. Keep in mind, however, if there is any doubt whatsoever in the RB's mind as to whether or not he should throw the ball, or if he just reads daylight, he should be running.

### Base Play Looks

Diagram 11-5 illustrates "Special-right hash-fly, pitch left"; while Diagram 11-6 shows "special-left hash-fly, pitch pass right." Keep in mind that if the SB comes into contact with a defender on the LOS in Diagram 11-6 he will hold his block.

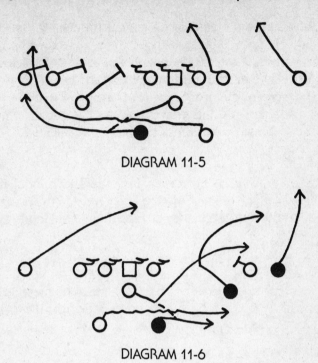

DIAGRAM 11-5

DIAGRAM 11-6

## PASS

### Play Objective

The basic attack principle here comes directly from the option air attack scheme. One of the key advantages of the special series is that it does not allow the defense to stack up against the run. The pass must be defended, and from this particular formation, that defense encounters added complications. The call in the huddle is "pass strong" or "pass quick," thereby determining the attack side. The line definitions here are the same as they are for the air option. This can easily and effectively be run with motion; fly has not really proven effective.

### Position Responsibilities and Blocking Patterns

*Line*

CENTER: NG, DG, offside versus gaps.

GUARDS: DG, offside versus gaps.

TACKLES: If strong end is in a hash alignment, the tackles block the DT, go offside versus gaps, but never double-team inside if the outside gap is threatened. If quick or strong is in a middle alignment, they drop two steps, and fake a screen attempt. Since the formation is odd enough to begin with, this may throw a little added concern the defense's way even if the tackle is ineligible.

## Set Backs

Key near the LB; if he comes, they attack him. If not, the backs aggressively attack the first man to show outside the guard's block. If there is no one to block, they flare as they would in the air option.

## Receivers

STRONG END:

*If onside:* Keys the LB to his side. If he fires, he runs the pop. If he doesn't, he runs a comeback from 12 to 10.

*If offside:* Drive.

SLOT BACK:

*If onside:* Keys the near LB. If he fires, pop. If not, jet.

*If offside:* Drive.

FLY:

SB executes his same responsibility to the other side of the formation, while the StE executes as the quick end normally would.

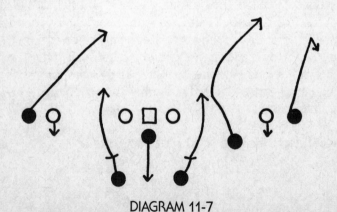

DIAGRAM 11-7

*Quarterback*

Executes exactly as he does in the air option. The QB draw ("go" call) has proven a nice weapon here.

## Base Play Look

Diagram 11-7 depicts "special-middle, pass quick."

## SCREEN

## Play Objective

While the pass is geared at keeping the defense honest, the effect of the special tends to have the defender responsible for underneath and deep pass coverage, either to hesitate, which helps open up the normal pass, or to drop very hard. If the drops are deep enough and the pass rush strong enough, the screen (strong or quick) can certainly be taken advantage of here. As on a pass call, mo can easily be used.

## Position Responsibilities and Blocking Patterns

The responsibilities here are exactly as they are in the pass, except for the following differences:

- The QB will set up as in the pass, but will fade deeper to hit his screen target.
- The screen back will set to block, and then slip in behind the C and the two guards. The offside back runs a deep flare if he has no one to block. If he does, he slips the block and looks for any "garbage" that might have read screen from the backfield.
- The C and guards block as always, but don't move their feet, thereby allowing the rush to penetrate. Once the ball is caught, the C takes the first defender to show in the middle of the field. The guards pick up the first man to show outside the center's block to his side.

## Base Play Look

Diagram 11-8 is "special-middle, screen strong."

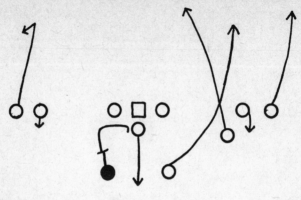

DIAGRAM 11-8

## Play Calling for the Special

The basic rule of thumb for play selection here is simple. To get the perimeter and passing game to open up, it is a must to force the defense to adequately defend the middle. If they don't, the sneak by itself will well prove the worth of the series.

The sneak will be run as the top priority play if (1) the C-G seams are uncovered, or (2) if there is no LB over the center or in the "onside" area. It doesn't matter whether or not the sneak is run as a huddle call, normal automatic, or "goose" automatic.

When the automatic system is used, it is done so with the QB keeping only two plays in mind—the sneak and one of the other four plays. If he doesn't have the sneak, he calls the "other" play.

## Use of Shifting in the Special

Shifting both to and from the special has also proven most effective. It is important that the QB keep his hash and automatic special alignment in mind when calling the shift in the huddle. The formation the QB wants the offense to begin in is given first and followed by the new formation. For example, "slot right-shift-special..." indicates that the offense would break the huddle and align in a slot right, and shift to the special on the QB's command. To go from the special to another formation would go something like this, "special-left hash-shift-slot right."

# 12

## Polishing Off
## the Perimeter Attack

A book on the perimeter attack would not be complete without a discussion and analysis of certain dimensions that complete the entire scheme's philosphy. Normally, such a "polishing off" of the offense would include material on a goal-line offense, both going in and coming out, a two-minute drill when behind, and a slow-down drill when ahead.

While this chapter will take a look at both a two-minute and slow-down drill, the actual goal-line offense is really the perimeter attack itself. While certain plays may seem more appropos than others, the offense itself has proven effective regardless of which end of the field it has found itself. One of the key reasons for this is the blocking patterns, which have been designed for each play. Whether a team uses a 6-5 or variation thereof, a 7-4, or a gap-8 look for goal-line purposes, it will be handled by the blocking pattern. Remember that the primary beauty of each blocking pattern is that it is an all-encompassing scheme that does not have to be adjusted for each game or for each defense. The pattern rule and defensive recognition calls made by the line will more than adequately handle any defensive look. While the inside game has proven effective in goal-line situations, the quality of the outside attack is the fact that most goal-line defenses tend to overplay the inside. If they do this the offense will score that way.

Besides the two-minute and slow-down drills to be discussed here, this chapter will include a look at a unique conversion philosophy, a play scheme called *"bingo,"* a comment on playing in bad weather, a come-from-behind philosophy, some general thoughts on play selection, and a closing note.

## A UNIQUE CONVERSION CONCEPT

### The Conversion Philosophy and Background

While differences exist in teams' conversion philosophies, most teams are pretty straightforward about theirs; namely, as long as you have a kicker who can respectably place a one-point conversion, and most decent football programs have such a commodity, then do so. The rationale behind this is simple enough; one "sure" point in the hand is better than a "maybe" two in the bush.

The point here, though, is not to go into detail in terms of analyzing other coaching philosophies, but instead to propose a conversion concept that at first glance might seem unacceptable to an experienced coach, and that is to always go for two points.

Going into my third year at the first school where I was head coach, we made an assumption—that we would successfully kick 100 percent of every PAT we attempted. Going for two points meant that we would have to be successful at least 50 percent of the time to at least equal the point output via the kick.

To do so, we felt we had to have a sound goal line or conversion offense—a play or play series that could *consistently* give us 3 yards. An option-designed, perimeter attack-type series, when properly executed, should provide the qualities we were looking for, and obviously, we felt we had such a series.

The key word here is *consistency.* We felt that we had to practice our conversion plays every day, and run a conversion attempt any time we scored in practice. We did both. Five minutes of team offense was devoted to our conversion play. It was also necessary to convince our team of the great importance attached to the conversion, as well as believe strongly in it ourselves. We felt if we did all these things we should have a decent shot at reaching our 50 percent success ratio.

These practices and ideas, coupled with the belief that our offense should be psychologically up and the defense psychologically down immediately after our offense scores, had a great deal to do with us deciding to go wholeheartedly with a two-point conversion, regardless of the score. The only exception would be if a penalty backed us up to the 8 or 18-yard line, in which case, we would kick.

The results were positive enough that I kept that philosophy throughout the rest of my high school career. I will one day put it into effect again at the college level.

| SEASON | NUMBER OF GAMES | NUMBER OF TDS | NUMBER OF TWO-POINT CON-VERSIONS | NUMBER OF TWO-POINT CON-VERSIONS | NUMBER POINTS VIA CON-VERSIONS | SUCCESS RATIO |
|---|---|---|---|---|---|---|
| AT SCHOOL I | | | | | | |
| SEASON II (8-1-0) | 9 | 31 | 31 | 21 | 42 | 71% |
| SEASON III (8-1-0) | 9 | 34 | 34 | 28 | 56 | 82% |
| AT SCHOOL II | | | | | | |
| SEASON I (1-8-1) | 10 | 20 | 20 | 9 | 18 | 45% |
| SEASON II (3-7-0) | 10 | 24 | 22 | 15 | 30 | 68% |
| SEASON III (6-4) | 11 | 31 | 30 | 21 | 42 | 70% |
| 5 YEAR TOTALS | 49 | 140 | 137 | 94 | 188 | 69% |

It is important to remember that, going into that first season when we first put our philosophy and scheme into practice, our goal was to achieve a 50 percent success ratio. Keep in mind that we assumed we would be successful 100 percent of the time via the kick.

During the five-year period noted above, had we kicked each time we went for two, we would have scored 137 points at a 100 percent success ratio. As it was, we scored 188 points, or over 31 extra touchdowns! I believe that record is an incredible one. The only year we had some problem was the first year starting at a new school. The three times we didn't go for two were due to problems with penalties, for which there is no excuse anyway.

## Actual Conversions Procedure

The following is the conversion procedure actually carried out each time we scored a TD:

1. The QB requests the ball be spotted by the official on the hash. The team aligns in a normal slot to the wide side; there is no huddle.

2. Once the team is set, the QB stands back to give the impression he is waiting for the team to be set, though the team sets as quickly as possible without hesitation. Since the ball is snapped on "set" about 35 percent of the time that our offense puts the ball in play, the defense must be primed for a quick snap count.

3. The SB uses his judgment to count the defenders on or off the LOS that are aligned head up or outside him. Our first priority in calling a play here is the Isotak sprint to the quick side. If there are four or more defenders aligned in that area, the SB will discretely signal to the QB that the play will not be run. If there are three or less, he signals that the play should be run.

4. The StE does the same thing to his side, except his magic number is three. Three or more means no; two or less means yes. His signal to the QB determines whether the second play in order of priority is going to be run. The second play is the Isotak sprint to the strong side.

5. As the QB gets set, he has already looked to the SB first and the StE second. If the SB signals "yes," he automatics to the Isotak sprint quick, which is first priority. If the signal is "no," and the StE says "yes," he automatics to Isotak sprint strong, which is the second priority. If the StE also signals "no," there are only four men between the SB and StE. The QB then automatics to the Isotak quick, which is the third of a three-set priority.

6. The QB may "goose" automatic if he sees a definite score here at his own discretion.

7. After the automatic is given, the set backs shift to an I on "set." The snap count will always be on "3."

8. If the defense goes offsides, we huddle up and go with the pitch or lead on "set," depending on what the call is. If we planned on Isotak sprint quick, we run the pitch to the quick side. If we planned on Isotak sprint strong, we run lead to the strong side. Before stepping under the C, the QB "reminds" the offense not to go offsides. This should give the defense the impression that the snap count is a late one.

## Play Descriptions and Variations

The Isotak is run just as explained in Chapter Eight. However, there are some variations on the Isotak sprint. Whether executed quick or strong, the entire line blocks as normal. In Isotak sprint quick, the quick end seals inside blocking the first man to show on the LOS. This simulates the run on the corner. The SB begins to release inside, but breaks to the flat moving with the QB, and gains depth for the far corner of the end zone. The strong back will run directly at the outside breast of the first man to show on the corner outside the QE's block. The quick back executes as normal; if he clears the LOS, which he shouldn't, he throttles down deep in the end zone on the onside hash. The StE begins to run a crossing pattern but comes under control and stops at his near hash. He gives the impression he is out of the play. Should the QB have to scramble back to him, he must be prepared to break to the short sideline.

If Isotak sprint strong is run, the StE executes as the SB does when he is onside, and the QE executes like the StE does when the StE is offside. The SB runs a crossing pattern here and throttles down on the onside hash deep in the end zone. If the quick back clears, he is to run an out just over the goal line.

Whether going strong or quick, the QB thinks run first as he attacks the corner at top speed. If all avenues to the goal line are blocked and he is forced to the sidelines, the QB may plant and "runaround" back to the formation. Remember that this is a conversion and there is nothing to lose if things don't work out. The offside end should be wide open by this time. However, this method is only a last resort for the QB; he wants to get the ball in the end zone normally, if he can.

Diagram 12-1 illustrates Isotak sprint quick in a conversion situation.

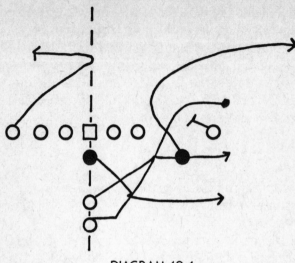

DIAGRAM 12-1

## Seeming Disadvantage to the Philosophy

The problem here becomes apparent the first time you lose a game by one or get tied, when the two-point conversion is missed. There are plenty of Monday morning quarterbacks sitting in the stands or writing for the papers ready to pounce on you for that.

However, when you lose a game 7-6, but scored first, is it not true that had you made the conversion, there would have been no possible way you could have lost that game? Would it not also be true that when you are successful going for two, aren't you putting your opponent in a position where he is also forced to go for two? Wouldn't it also then be true that since your opponent probably doesn't have the same philosophy, they wouldn't be so proficient as you? Let's assume you kicked successfully for one point. Would not the trailing team still be in position to beat you later in the game? While criticism at times may come heavy for not kicking, I would honestly question its validity.

To take it a step further, let's analyze the following situation: you were trailing, but just tied the score at 20-20. There are five seconds left in the game. Do you kick or go for two?

I am well aware that 19 of 20 of the most respected coaches in the country would say kick, but according to this conversion philosophy, I would still go for two. I firmly believe that the only reason why our two-point philosophy is so successful is because of the emphasis placed on it, and the work put into it. Our kids and staff know ahead of time that whenever we score, we are going for two—period. We brainwashed ourselves to the point where our staff and players did not want to kick an extra point, and it is in large part due to this "brainwashing" that we proved so successful.

Let's get back to the "20-20 score and five seconds left in the game" situation just cited. In every critical situation all season, we have gone for two. We are experienced and successful at it. Do we now put our place kick team on the field in that situation, and expect a *sure* one-pointer from them?

What happens when you score once again at the very end of the game, but are down 20-19 or 20-18? Would not the fact that you have always gone for two in situations like that, make you much better prepared to handle those two points so desperately needed now? Doesn't the defense have extra to prepare for in practice?

At the very least, the two-point conversion philosophy discussed here is food for thought.

## BINGO

Whenever in our normal offensive huddle call, a *"bingo"* is added to the play, the offense immediately runs our conversion procedure if a first down is made. If a first down is not made, the "bingo" is ignored. While the QB has to be careful in regards to which hash his team may wind up on, it is a rather effective tool to use in the normal field of play. Going without a huddle at certain times for no apparent reason has to become a little disconcerting to the defense, and it gives them extra to prepare for. The added preparation for the offense is truly minimal.

## THE PERIMETER ATTACK TWO-MINUTE DRILL

Many games are won or lost in the last seconds or minutes of play. With time running out in the half or game, something must be done to conserve time and still move the ball. Once again, priority has to be given to a scheme where little extra need be taught.

## Procedure for Two-Minute Drill

1. Know when the clock stops. Every coach and player *must* know when the clock stops until the start of the next play, or temporarily. This is not a nicety, it is a necessity.

2. Know how many time-outs you are allotted. Every coach and player must also know this. These must be kept track of during the game.

3. *Only* the QB calls time-out. He will completely control what goes on the field. In general, it may not matter who calls time-out, but it does during this drill.

4. The team will line up or huddle up on the QB's command. If the clock has stopped permanently, the QB will command the team to huddle. If the clock hasn't, the QB will command an alignment, generally, a slot to the wide side, depending on that week's game plan.

5. When the team huddles, a play is called. When the team lines up, there is a predetermined play run. This play is determined with the game plan that week. The players are not asked to remember more than one play at a time; and if there is no huddle, the ball will be snapped on "set." The play used is generally the sprint or air option.

6. When the play that was just run stops the clock, the QB calls a huddle. If not, he calls the formation, and the procedure is repeated.

7. As the half or game draws dangerously to its end, the situation is called *"crisis."* Once "crisis" is determined, the QB will call a time-out whenever the clock does not stop. When it stops temporarily, he lines the team up; when it stops permanently, he huddles up.

8. A general rule of thumb for all ballcarriers is that if you can't get quality extra yardage, get out of bounds; unless, of course, that extra yard or two means a first down or a score.

9. Break up all pileups quickly. You can't control how the defense moves after the whistle, but you can control the offense.

10. *Hustle! Hustle! Hustle!*

## THE SLOW DOWN

The principle behind the *slow down* is the same as the two-minute drill, except now the offense is ahead by 8 points or less. Here the objective is to use up as much time as possible in attainment of first downs. This would take place any time in the fourth quarter.

### Procedure for the Slow Down

1. Know how much time the offense is allowed to get the ball off. Use those seconds.
2. No time-outs may be called by anyone for any reason.
3. The team will now break the pileups slowly.
4. Never allow yourself to be driven out of bounds.
5. Above all, think *ball.* Never, never allow a turnover here!

## A COMMENT ON THE WEATHER

While it is important to be aware of the weather in football, a mistake some coaches and some people in general make is to worry about things that they can't control. Again, while any good coach will both be prepared for and be able to adapt to bad weather, he can't control it.

The perimeter attack can attack inside with power and authority, making the best use of blocking angles, and outside with speed and options. A great team can play under lousy conditions and win. Prepare for the bad weather, but don't worry about it.

## COME-FROM-BEHIND PHILOSOPHY

There is nothing unique about my feelings here. There are few things sweeter in this life for a football coach than coming from behind for the victory.

When a team is down, it has to come up with everything it has to pull together mentally, physically, and emotionally. It has to turn into a human machine. It takes a team with real character and pride to hang in there when the going gets rough.

The perimeter attack has always been an explosive, while consistent, offense. While that type of offense is needed, it takes men with character to come from behind in football, not a lot of fancy theory.

## SOME SIMPLE THOUGHTS ON PLAY SELECTION

An entire book can be devoted to this topic alone. My purpose here is to discuss in general not so much why or when each play in the perimeter attack would be called, but what areas of the defense should be attacked.

Throughout this text, thought was given to the purpose of each play, and how the play could be utilized in an overall offensive attack in the play objective. In the previous chapter, time was also spent on what plays could be called in the special—*when* and *why.* A similar process was referred to in the discussion of the conversion philosophy.

The purpose now is to be as general as possible, for there are just too many variables involved. Actual play selection in a game is based on a well thought out and organized game plan, which would include a multitude of tendency analyses, opponents' personnel evaluation, and a breakdown of their defensive philosophy with their strengths and weaknesses. Play selection is also based on experience and instincts.

Once the game starts, however, the types of things my staff looks for primarily comes down to counting the defense. Splitting the nose of the center right down the center of the defense, we count the number of defenders to our quick side and the number to our strong side. Anyone *directly* over the C, like a NG, MLB, or safety, count as one-half. If the defense is balanced, we expect six people to our quick side and five to our strong. If the ball is on the hash, we count the sideline as a defender if we are planning to attack the perimeter. If the count comes to less than five defenders to the strong side, or less than six to the quick side, that is the side we attack. If the numbers stay balanced, namely six-quick and five-strong, we attack the wide side.

Once the side is determined, we then count the number of defenders on or off the LOS, outside the QT's or StT's position. The key numbers here are three and two, respectively. If there are three or less defenders outside that QT, the attack area is the defensive perimeter. If there are four or more, the inside is dealt with. To the strong side, the attack area will be the perimeter if there are two or less defenders outside the StT. It will be the interior if there are three or more.

## A PERSONAL NOTE

Of all the football books, journals, and clinics I have read or attended, the vast majority have proven of some value in the development of my own philosophy, program, system, and organization. I have seldom read or listened to another coach without coming away with at least some ideas to spark my own thinking, even if sometimes it might be what not to do.

In a nutshell, this has really been the purpose of this book; to provide a stimulus for thought. As stated in the introduction, if a coach can digest this book in part or in its entirety, and come away with a thought or two that will help him in his own preparation, organization, or philosophy, the book will have been a success.

Certainly, there are still many coaches around who firmly believe that the game hasn't changed at all over the last 25 years, and that the game will always be won by the team who makes the fewest mistakes, and does the best job of blocking, tackling, and running. The irony here, though, is that there isn't a high school, college, or pro coach in the country who wouldn't wholeheartedly agree that excellence of execution, along with quality personnel, wins games.

To say that, however, doesn't mean the game hasn't changed. There is a much greater emphasis on detail today than ever before. That emphasis on design, technique, and organization seems to increase from year to year. While the actual game of football itself hasn't changed, the design and detail within which the systems execute, has.

The problem with this or any book is a common one. No matter how intricate an explanation of a point becomes, it may still need clarification. I have learned a great deal of football through an exchange of ideas with others. The objective of this book is to get you thinking. If you have a question about any of the points or concepts developed in this book, feel free to contact me for a further clarification. I know that might seem a little unrealistic, but I don't believe it is. You can find my name in the Annual Directory of the American Football Coaches Association.

In closing, I would like to leave you with a thought, quoted from the late Red Blaik of Army: "Victory is often achieved by inches, timed in seconds, and denied through mistakes. A man learns, through sweat and sacrifice, that he can overcome these mistakes. For the real champion, the joy of victory is ample reward for the hardships of training." Keep this in mind when things get tough.

# Index